D1359904

Personnel Economics

The Wicksell Lectures

GEORGE SMILEY MEMORIAL LIBRARY
CENTRAL METHODIST COLLEGE
FAYETTE, MISSOURI 65248

HF
5549
,L32
1995

Personnel Economics

Edward P. Lazear

The MIT Press
Cambridge, Massachusetts
London, England

Second printing, 1996

© 1995 Massachusetts Institute of Technology

All rights reserved. No part of this book may be reproduced in any form by any electronic or mechanical means (including photocopying, recording, or information storage and retrieval) without permission in writing from the publisher.

This book was set in Palatino by Asco Trade Typesetting Ltd., Hong Kong and was printed and bound in the United States of America.

Library of Congress Cataloging-in-Publication Data

Lazear, Edward P.
  Personnel economics / Edward P. Lazear.
    p.   cm. — (The Wicksell lectures ; 1993)
  Includes bibliographical references and index.
  ISBN 0-262-12188-3 (hc : alk. paper)
  1. Personnel management. 2. Economics. I. Title. II. Series.
HF5549.L32   1995
658.3—dc20   95-17411
                                                                        CIP

The Wicksell Lectures

The 1958 The Wicksell Lecture Society, in cooperation with the Social Science Institute of Stockholm University, the Stockholm School of Economics, and the Swedish Economic Association, inaugurated a series of lectures to honor the memory of Knut Wicksell (1851–1926). Until 1975 lectures were given each year. After a period of dormancy the series was reinaugurated in 1979 by the Swedish Economic Association. Starting with the 1982 lectures, a set of lectures has been offered every two years.

Contents

Preface

When Eskil Wadensjö invited me to give the 1993 Wicksell Lectures, he suggested that I discuss my work on what has come to be called "personnel economics." The book that follows is an expanded version of those lectures. In this book, I do not purport to summarize the entire field. In particular, there is a great deal of important research by other scholars that is only mentioned or not discussed at all. The lectures were intended to focus somewhat heavily on my own work and the following chapters unabashedly overweight my own contributions. The issues addressed below form the basis of what is most central to the graduate level courses that I taught at the University of Chicago and that I now teach at Stanford.

The material contained herein is only mildly technical. Most of the details behind the analyses are found in the papers on which the discussions are based. The equations that are presented are skeletons of the underlying theories. The level and style of presentation is intended to introduce scholars in other subfields of economics, graduate students, and advanced undergraduates to personnel economics. As I will argue below, the issues that have historically been in the domain of personnel analysts are of utmost importance in modern business. These topics can be brought into sharper focus by applying the tools of modern economic theory. In this book, I hope to convince the reader that the personnel related questions are worth asking and that economists can provide the correct answers to those questions.

Acknowledgment

I thank the Swedish Economics Association and the Stockholm School of Economics for giving me the opportunity to present my thoughts on personnel economics in the 1993 Wicksell Lectures. I especially thank Eskil Wadensjö, President of the Swedish Economic Association and my hosts at the Stockholm School of Economics, Lars Bergman, Staffan Burenstam Linder, and Karl Jungenfelt, for their kind hospitality and for providing me with a stimulating group of colleagues during my visit. I am also indebted to Canice Prendergast, John Roberts, and Sherwin Rosen for providing comments on earlier drafts of these lectures.

Personnel Economics

1   Introduction

What Is "the Economics of Personnel"?

Personnel is defined by a well-known text as "obtaining, organizing and motivating the human resources required by enterprise."[1] Being an applied field, personnel currently includes topics like hiring and firing, training, compensation methods, job design and worker evaluation. At some level these topics are familiar to mainstream economists. The theory of production describes how much labor is to be hired, how it should be coupled with capital, how its use should vary with wages, and so forth. But in standard production theory the level of abstraction typically is far too high to be of much use to practitioners. As a result the field has been dominated by industrial psychologists and sociologists.

There are many questions that cannot be answered by the most abstract and general models. Structure must be added to provide the kind of detail necessary for a useful theory. For example, traditional production theory says nothing about how to structure wages so as to motivate workers best. Agency theory comes closer to answering the specific questions, but it also comes up short.[2] A manager who reads the agency literature would have a difficult time determining the ideal commission rate for a salesperson, even if he could make his way through the material. Personnel economics attempts to fill the gap.

I do not view the role of personnel analysis as one of translation. Instead, it is to bring the theory to the level of details, so that much more specific predictions and prescriptions can be made. In this lecture I will try to point out the ways in which standard economic theory has been used to address the personnel issues that arise in business on a daily basis.

Why Call It the "Economics of Personnel" Instead of "Personnel"?

Traditional analyses of personnel issues have been quite successful in out-
lining the problems, though much less successful at providing solutions to
them. Economists have a comparative advantage in providing solutions
but a comparative disadvantage in asking questions. The strength of economic theory is that it is rigorous and analytic. It follows the scientific
method, much like physics and biology. But the weakness of economics is
that to be rigorous, simplifying assumptions must be made that constrain
the analysis and narrow the focus of the researcher. It is for this reason that
the broader-thinking industrial psychologists and sociologists are better at
identifying issues but worse at providing answers. Our narrowness allows
us to provide concrete solutions, but sometimes it prevents us from thinking about the larger or more important features of the problem.

The textbook mentioned above states, "there are no universal objec-
tives just as there are no absolute principles governing personnel policies
and practices."[3] I totally reject that view and argue that the economics of
personnel is a science devoted to the discovery of those policies and principles that describe the way the world does or should behave.

This point of course is not specific to the economics of personnel. It is
common for noneconomists to decry generalization, or at least our form of
it. The economist views generalization as the goal. Theories are successful
only when their applicability is broad and their content important. While
not specific to personnel issues, the suggestion by noneconomists that
generalization is impossible is more likely to be applied to human resources issues than to more impersonal market structures. After all, workers are individuals, unlike pieces of capital, and they have idiosyncratic
backgrounds and behavior patterns. The task of personnel economists is to
find simple models that do well in describing important components of
worker behavior.

Four Themes

Throughout these lectures, I will emphasize four themes:

First, personnel economics is largely normative, but it remains systematic. Since the analysis is appropriate for applied business situations, it can
be taught as a prescriptive science as well as a descriptive one.

Second, a personnel system is an entire structure that can be understood
within the economic framework. Since it is an entire structure, it makes no

sense to analyze one part without considering other parts. For example, benefit levels cannot be determined in the absence of compensation considerations despite the attempt by most firms to separate their benefits and compensation departments. Nor can the pay that goes to a vice-president be evaluated without examining the pay of an assistant vice-president in the same firm. Theory and empirical evidence link these components.

Third, much of the essence of personnel economics depends on relative comparisons rather than on absolute ones. Individuals are compared to one another rather than to some absolute standard. Similarly firms are compared to one another and are not judged on the basis of some absolute criterion.

Relative comparisons are more important than absolute standards in many contexts.[4] Often it matters not so much whether something is good but rather whether it is better than what another firm or worker has to offer. The economics of personnel is full of examples where relative comparisons reign. Tournament theory occupies a significant part of the following discussion, but it is only the most obvious of the relative comparison models. In the context of institutional considerations, particularly those that relate to the law, relative comparisons rather than absolute standards are central to most issues. These themes recur throughout the course of these lectures, and I will attempt to emphasize them when they are relevant.

Fourth, economics is well suited to the study of micro-level human relations. While psychology and sociology may be able to offer insights into an individual's behavior at work, these fields have nothing over economics in their ability to analyze human issues that are difficult to quantify. On the contrary, economics reveals that seemingly straightforward and intuitive explanations of work-related phenomena are often misleading and frequently wrong. There is no reason to cede control over this area of social science to other fields merely because they involve human emotion.

The Substance of the Economics of Personnel

Theories of Compensation

Much of the literature that comes under the rubric of the economics of personnel relates most directly to compensation. Methods of pay and specific formulas are the focus of a large part of the work in the area. There is good reason: As important as worker compensation is, there has until recently been no underlying theory of compensation. The standard model is that of competition. Workers are assumed to be paid the competitive wage because the labor market is large and impersonal. But the form in which the competitive wage is paid, its structure over the worker's life cycle, and its relation to the job or hierarchical position in the firm are topics that have been largely unexplored until recently.[5]

Two points are important: First, compensation must be treated as an entire structure, not as a collection of separately determined components. The wage of a vice-president cannot be set independent of the wage of an assistant vice-president because the vice-president's wage affects the desire of all those below him to obtain the job. Thus it is misguided to examine the wage level of one type of employee to determine its correctness without placing it in the context of the entire hierarchy. Tournament theory, discussed in chapter 3, and life-cycle incentive models are, in my view, the best way to rationalize the entire firm's compensation structure.

Second, economic theories are fully capable of integrating all aspects of compensation into the models. It is not necessary that remuneration take pecuniary forms. Psychic income that derives from job amenities, status, working conditions, and other factors are easily incorporated into the standard analysis. What distinguishes the economic approach from that of other disciplines is that the nonpecuniary components are converted into their monetary equivalents in the course of the analysis. As a result economists can discuss these factors in concrete and rigorous fashion.

Job Design and Job Definition

Standard economic theory places no importance on the notion of a "job." In the theory of production there is only labor and capital, and both are treated as continuous variables. But every human resources manager thinks of the job as a crucial unit of analysis. Personnel economics places a heavy, albeit sometimes implicit, weight on the job per se. Jobs have different meanings and carry different connotations in the various theories, but jobs are at the heart of many analyses.

Somewhat less developed is the area of job design. While many theories are quite explicit about jobs, few have discussed the ways in which jobs are constructed. In part, the lingering abstractness of the models is to blame. But a more direct cause is lack of good data on which to base and test theories. As more data become available, economists will say more about the specifics of job design.

Institutional Aspects of the Employment Relationship

Usually, when economists speak of institutions as being important, they are referring to nonprice mechanisms for resource allocation. There are many institutions that are important in personnel relations. Mandatory retirement, which forces workers to leave the job when they reach a specified age, is one of the first institutions that I analyze. Mandatory retirement is an institution because it is a quantity rather than price mechanism designed to affect behavior.

There are other related institutions. Tenure among academics, up-or-out promotion schemes in the military, and job security arrangements are institutions that use quantity rather than price mechanisms to bring about a desired result. Some of the literature in the economics of personnel fits into this category and will be discussed below.

Other institutions directly govern the balance of power between workers and management. Countries differ in the managerial roles that they ascribe to labor. These roles are not priced directly, though the rules may have implications for the price at which labor is traded. Unions, works councils, quality circles, and other aspects of worker entry into corporate governance fall into this category.

Training

As a result of the work of Becker, Mincer, and others, economic research on worker training is quite developed.[6] While there are few studies that document explicit training programs, there is an enormous literature that examines the effects of training on wages and worker turnover. More recently other life-cycle theories of wage growth have provided alternative explanations for observed patterns. The provision of incentives may involve payment over time that resembles the path generated by the accumulation of skills on the job.

At the positive level, researchers have been trying to find ways to differentiate observationally between the two theories. At the normative level, there is much less of a problem. Few doubt that on-the-job training is an important part of the job environment. Also most accept that wage increases associated with performance serve to motivate workers. Thus personnel economics is quite capable of integrating the two theories into one prescriptive package.

Evaluation

Worker evaluation is an important part of the industrial environment. Most firms engage in some sort of evaluation process on a periodic basis. For academics formal evaluations occur infrequently over the worker's career. In most universities serious evaluations are conducted only occasionally. What explains the difference in evaluation behavior across firms and worker types? What aspects of the worker are evaluated? Is it worker ability, worker effort, or worker output, measured as quantity or quality, that is most relevant?

Related firms often devote resources to evaluating the job in addition to evaluating the worker who occupies it. An entire industry has grown up to perform job evaluation, where large data sets are collected so that one firm can compare its treatment of workers in a particular job to that given by the rest of the market. The theory behind such comparisons exists, and it has definite implications for the uses to which such evaluation techniques can be put.

The Law and Other Institutions

In Europe the law has long played an active role in labor markets. The U.S. government has adopted a less interventionist posture until recently. Now state and federal governments have become more aggressive in their regulation of labor markets.

How do firms respond to regulation? What can be said at a normative level to assist businesses in thinking about their responses to particular regulations?

The Role of Business School Economists

My career started in the University of Chicago's Economics Department, but I have been an economist in a business school for about fifteen years. Moving to a business school had a profound effect on the nature of my research, and I believe that some discussion of the business school environment is relevant to understanding personnel economics.

It is not by accident that the economics of personnel was developed in large part by business school economists. Teaching in a business school forces an economist to deal with questions at a much more applied level. But this does not require forfeiture of analytic skills nor academic respectability.

Business school economists differ from their economics department counterparts in two ways. First, the problems that business school economists are induced to focus on are more applied and less abstract. Second, in a business school, analyses and applications are not only positive but also somewhat normative. The first difference will become apparent during the course of these lectures, since the specifics are the essence of this book. But before jumping to these specifics, it is useful to digress for a few moments to discuss the normative aspects of the problem.

Normative and Positive Economics

Milton Friedman (1953) describes the manner in which most economists think about the world in his essay on positive economics. He argues that the scientific value of economics is its ability to predict the world as we see it. Those of us who teach economics to businesspersons must take the positive analysis and make it prescriptive. But therein lies an inherent contradiction: If the theory is a good description of the real world, then businesses must already operate in the ways we describe. If so, then they are teaching us, rather than the reverse. A good positive theory is a description of what is, and this precludes a role for those who want to teach it to others as a behavior ideal. At the extreme a positive theory that explains the world perfectly leaves no room for a normative economist to improve the situation.

Alternatively, we can argue that businesses do not behave according to our models but should. Were they to adopt our methods, their output and profits would be higher. If this assertion is true, there is a definite role for the normative economist but a much less important one for economics in describing the world. At the extreme all firms could be educated so as to improve profits, but then none would behave in accordance with the predictions of the positive theory. How can the two positions be reconciled so that we can retain our claim to be scientists but still teach economics to business students as a prescriptive model?

The answer lies in the middle ground. While economics may do very well at explaining most of what goes on in the world, some economic agents may not behave as they should. Putting these individuals on the right path can be socially productive. Without economists the discipline of the market would cause the errant firms to fail. Economists can remedy the situation more rapidly by increasing the proportion of successes. But even in the absence of such intervention by economics teachers, the theory may do quite well at explaining not only what should be but also what is.

To see this, consider a particular example. Let us suppose that firms are choosing between two compensation schemes for their workers. One scheme provides correct motivation, whereas the other does not. A new firm selects the correct scheme γ of the time. After one period the errant firms go out of business and are replaced by new firms, which select the right compensation scheme γ of the time. Naturally all firms that choose the correct scheme survive. Firms that choose the correct scheme have normalized output level of one unit. Firms that choose the incorrect scheme have output levels of $(1 - \theta)$ units.

Suppose that an industry survives for ten periods and then perishes. In period 1, γ of the firms choose the correct scheme and $1 - \gamma$ choose the wrong scheme. In period 2 those who chose incorrectly during the first period are replaced by new firms. Thus in period 2 the proportion with the correct scheme is

$$P_2 = \gamma + (1 - \gamma)\gamma$$

$$= P_1 + (1 - P_1)\gamma,$$

where P_t is the proportion with the correct scheme in period t. In general, P_t can be defined recursively as

$$P_t = P_{t-1} + (1 - P_{t-1})\gamma. \tag{1.1}$$

For industries that start up uniformly over time, in steady state there are as many industries in period 1 as there are in period 2, ..., as in period T (in this case, ten). Thus the proportion of firms in the economy that are operating with the correct compensation scheme is simply

$$\frac{1}{T} \sum_{t=1}^{T} P \tag{1.2}$$

because $1/T$ industries are in period 1, $1/T$ are in period 2, and so forth. Output for the typical firm in the economy is then

$$\frac{1}{T} \sum_{t=1}^{T} [P_t + (1 - P_t)(1 - \theta)], \tag{1.3}$$

since P_t of the firms produce 1 and $1 - P_t$ produce $1 - \theta$ at any point in time.

Suppose that $\gamma = 0.5$ so that new firms are just as likely to choose the wrong compensation scheme as the right one. Further suppose that choosing the wrong compensation scheme reduces the firm's output by 10 per-

Table 1.1
An example of normative and positive economics

Period	Proportion correct	Output
A. Without economist's help ($\gamma = 0.5000$, $\theta = 0.1000$)		
1	0.5000	0.9500
2	0.7500	0.9750
3	0.8750	0.9875
4	0.9375	0.9938
5	0.9688	0.9969
6	0.9844	0.9984
7	0.9922	0.9992
8	0.9961	0.9996
9	0.9980	0.9998
10	0.9990	0.9999
Economy	0.9001	0.99001
B. With economist's help ($\gamma = 0.501$, $\theta = 0.100$)		
1	0.5010	0.9501
2	0.7510	0.9751
3	0.8757	0.9876
4	0.9380	0.9938
5	0.9691	0.9969
6	0.9846	0.9985
7	0.9923	0.9992
8	0.9962	0.9996
9	0.9981	0.9998
10	0.9990	0.9999
Economy	0.9005	0.99005

Note: Economist increases GDP by 0.00004. In the United States this would be about $198,441,919.

cent (i.e., $\theta = 0.1$). Table 1.1 shows how the average firm's output and the proportion of firms that have the correct scheme vary with the maturity of the industry.

First, note that convergence is very quick. Even with half of the new firms choosing the wrong scheme, 88 percent of the firms in an industry are using the correct compensation scheme by the third period. By period 7, 99 percent of the firms use the appropriate compensation scheme.

Using equation (1.2) in steady state, 90 percent of all firms in the economy have the right compensation scheme. Thus a good positive theory, which assumes that firms behaved optimally, would do a good job at predicting the behavior of the typical firm. The theory would be correct 90 percent of the time.

But this does not mean that there is no role for the normative economist. To see this, suppose that an economist can raise the proportion of firms who choose the correct compensation scheme from 0.5 to 0.501, namely the economist affects one in one thousand firms. Panel B of the table shows that the effect on the time path of learning is imperceptible, but there is a significant effect on aggregate output.

Substitution of the relevant numbers into (1.3) yields output per average firm of 0.90001. That is, before any intervention by the economics community, $\gamma = 0.5$ and

$$\frac{1}{10} \sum_{t=1}^{10} [P_t + (1 - P_t)(0.9)] = 0.90001.$$

With economists' intervention, γ rises to 0.501, and (1.3) yields output per average firm of 0.90005:

$$\frac{1}{10} \sum_{t=1}^{10} [P_t + (1 - P_t)(0.9)] = 0.90005.$$

Intervention brings about a 4/1000 of a percent increase in GDP. Applied to the United States, this means about $200 million, which probably surpasses the cost of teaching economics in business schools.[7]

It is quite easy to construct examples where most of the world behaves as predicted by optimizing models in equilibrium but where there is ample room for beneficial effects of economic education. This example reveals that it is not very difficult to construct scenarios in which economic conclusions derived from specifically optimizing models, which ignore any errors, do a good job of predicting outcomes. But it also illustrates that prescriptive analysis can greatly increase productivity, even when few firms are making errors. The example also illustrates that while a great deal of guessing may occur by any particular firm, in equilibrium the vast majority of firms continue to do the right thing. In this example every firm flips a fair coin at the outset. Each firm has only a 50 percent chance of choosing the correct compensation scheme. Yet in equilibrium 90 percent of the firms in the economy are choosing the correct compensation scheme. Nor were the numbers that brought about this particular outcome especially unrealistic.

Organization of the Lectures

Since much of the work to date in the economics of personnel is on compensation, a large part of these lectures is devoted to specific theories of compensation. Compensation encompasses a wide variety of subtopics, and worker motivation, selection, and teamwork are central to the discussion. Thus compensation is discussed first.

The next part of the lectures discusses job design and the basic concept of a job. Where does the notion of a "job" fit into the economic framework, and how does thinking in terms of jobs affect what firms do? While it may seem more natural for the discussion of jobs to precede the rest of the material, it is difficult to discuss jobs in the absence of other theories of compensation, and so I begin with those theories.

After jobs have been defined, they can be evaluated. Thus the next section examines job and worker evaluation processes. Attention then turns to institutional arrangements, specifically, the law, codetermination and the industrial environment, and process considerations. Finally, some new areas of research are outlined and some rudimentary models are laid out.

2   Fixed or Variable Pay?

Variable pay simply means tying a worker's compensation to some output-based measure of performance. Fixed pay means that the worker's compensation is independent of output, often because output is difficult to measure or define, or because variations in output are affected primarily by factors over which the worker has no control.

In the real world there are many forms of variable pay. Indeed it is possible to argue that almost no job's pay is truly fixed. Poor performance over a substantial period of time results in lower future pay and, at the extreme, termination. Let us begin with the most basic form of variable pay, namely the piece rate.

Piece Rate Pay

Before asking whether the firm should compensate its workers according to a piece rate scheme, let us first derive the optimal scheme for a worker who is risk neutral.[1] Optimal schemes must accomplish two things, that is, they must achieve efficiency on two margins. First, they must induce a given worker to put forth the appropriate level of effort. Second, they must induce the right workers to come to work for the firm. Under risk neutrality the optimal payment scheme is a linear one, achieving the first-best level of effort.

To see this, consider the problem of a firm that is attempting to decide on the commission rate to give to a salesperson. The firm wants to maximize profits, but it must pay the worker enough to induce him to work for the firm. The problem can be broken into two stages. The first stage is labor supply: It is necessary to determine what level of effort or number of hours of work a worker will supply given some structure of compensation. Then, given the worker's labor supply behavior, the firm must choose the compensation formula that maximizes profits.

Let the firm pay on the basis of output according to the scheme

$$\text{Pay} = \alpha + \beta q, \tag{2.1}$$

where q is output and α and β are compensation parameters to be chosen by the firm. Output depends on effort and luck. Normalize the measurement of effort so that one unit of effort produces one unit of output. Then

$$q = e + v,$$

where v measures luck or measurement error.

The worker likes income but hates work, and his distaste for work is given by $C(e)$, where both C' and C'' are positive. The conditions C', $C'' > 0$ guarantee that the solution implies finite effort levels. These are not assumptions but rather empirical dicta. At some point the cost of producing an additional unit of expected output becomes infinite as the worker reaches complete exhaustion.

The worker's labor supply function is the solution to

$$\text{Max}_{e} \; E[\alpha + \beta(e + v)] - C(e), \tag{2.2}$$

with first-order condition

$$C'(e) = \beta. \tag{2.3}$$

Equation (2.3) is the worker's labor supply function, which the firm takes as given when it maximizes profits by choosing the parameters α and β. Given $C'' > 0$ and risk neutrality, effort increases in β. Higher "wage rates" induce more effort or hours of work, so labor supply functions are positively sloped. The firm's problem is

$$\text{Max}_{\alpha, \beta} \; E(q) - (\alpha + \beta e),$$

or   (2.4)

$$\text{Max}_{\alpha, \beta} \; e - (\alpha + \beta e)$$

subject to the individual rationality constraint that the worker is willing to take the job in the first place. Required is that

$$\alpha + \beta e \geq C(e). \tag{2.5}$$

Equation (2.5) merely says that the worker must earn enough to cover his disutility at the equilibrium level of effort. Substitution of (2.5) into (2.4) yields

$$\text{Max } e - C(e), \qquad (2.6)$$
$$\scriptstyle \alpha, \beta$$

with the first-order condition

$$\frac{\partial}{\partial \beta} = [1 - C'(e)]\frac{\partial e}{\partial \beta} = 0. \qquad (2.7)$$

($\partial e/\partial \alpha = 0$, so the second condition is redundant.)

Equation (2.7) implies that the firm will choose β so as to bring about efficiency. The firm, in its quest for profit, induces the worker to set the marginal cost of effort equal to its marginal social value of effort, in this case 1. Equations (2.3) and (2.7) taken together imply that $\beta = 1$. After β is chosen, the optimum level of effort is determined by (2.3); (2.5) then dictates the size of α necessary to attract the worker to the firm.

The fact that $\beta = 1$ implies that piece rate workers should be entitled to the entire residual profit. The firm merely "rents" the worker the job at price $-\alpha$ and then gives the worker the full output. The value to paying a worker 100 percent of the residual is illustrated by a taxicab example. There are many ways to pay taxi drivers. One possibility is to rent them the cab and allow them to keep everything that they make for themselves after having paid the rental. This is the scheme that has just been shown to be optimal. An alternative is to give them the cab and take 50 percent of the meter. The second scheme has a couple of problems. Among the most obvious is that since the company cannot monitor the amount of driving done, the cabby and passenger can make a deal to pay 75 percent of what the meter would show and make the trip with the meter off. Both passenger and cabby are better off at the expense of the company. When the meter is off, the cab's "for hire" sign is lighted so that the company can detect cheating. Still this is costly, and it provides a rationale for making the driver the complete residual claimant.

Another rationale, and the one on which I focus now, is that a 50 percent commission rate induces insufficient effort by the driver. Consider a taxi driver who has been working for eleven hours in a particular day and is trying to decide to whether to drive the cab for a twelfth hour. He reasons that if he drives the cab, he expects to pick up $10 in cab fare that hour. Let's suppose that he values the leisure associated with that twelfth hour of work at $8. That is, at any price greater than $8, the taxicab driver would be willing to put forth the effort and drive the cab. It is clearly efficient for the driver to work during that twelfth hour. The value of driving the twelfth hour is measured by the price that people are willing to pay for the services (in this case $10). The social cost associated with driving that twelfth hour is the driver's reservation wage, in this case $8. Since 10 exceeds 8, the driver should drive the cab. Put alternatively, both the cab company and the driver can be made better off by having the driver work the twelfth hour. Since the cab company takes in, at most, $10 in revenue and the driver requires, at least, $8 of compensation, deals can be struck that will make both parties happy and will induce the cab driver to drive the cab. But splitting the revenues is not one of them.

Suppose that the cab driver takes home 50 percent of his compensation and does not pay any rental on the cab. In this case the driver will quit and will not supply the twelfth hour of effort. Since he takes home only half of the $10 fare and since his reservation wage is $8, he prefers the leisure to the $5 of revenue. This is the standard intuition behind the rule that says a worker must be made a full residual claimant in order to induce him to put forth the efficient amount of effort.

There is another reason to make the worker receive the full marginal output, which has nothing to do with effort.[2] If workers differ in their characteristics, then paying a worker less than the full amount will cause adverse selection problems in the hiring process. The wrong workers will want to work at the firm.

Suppose that workers have different ability levels, indexed by q, which signify the level of output that they can produce. Let one firm pay according to the optimal formula derived above:

$$\text{Pay} = a + q.$$

Let another pay at a rate $b < 1$ for every dollar of output, but let it offer a (potentially) higher base wage, a'.[3] The situation is shown in figure 2.1.

All those workers with $q < q^*$ prefer the low piece rate firm, namely the one that sets $b < 1$ but sets $a' > a$. All those with $q > q^*$ prefer the high piece rate firm. Thus the best (and most profitable) workers go to the high piece rate firm, while the low-quality workers choose the firm with a higher base salary and lower commission rate.

It is necessarily the case that the firm makes more money on workers whose ability exceeds q^* than those whose ability is less than q^* when the compensation schemes are given by $a' + bq$ for low-ability workers and $a + q$ for high-ability workers. As long as there is free entry into the industry, firms cannot receive any rents ex post. In equilibrium, firms that pay $a + q$ will have to set a equal to minus the rental price on capital. The $|a|$ cannot exceed the rental price of capital, or workers could be stolen away by other firms that charge only $-a$ for the capital. Now consider firms that are charging only a' for the job. The worker's output, net of

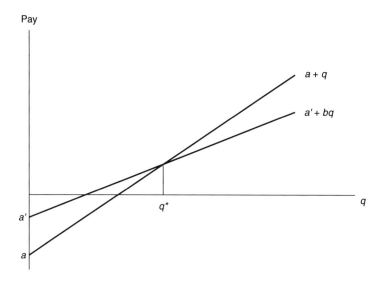

Figure 2.1

capital cost, is measured by $a + q$, but the worker is receiving $a' + bq$. In the region where q is less than q^*, $a' + bq$ exceeds $a + q$, which means that the worker is being paid more than his net output. Thus all firms are losing money on workers up to q^*. For workers whose output exceeds q^*, firms that paid $a' + bq$ would do better if they were able to attract the workers. Unfortunately, if some firms offer $a + q$ (which in equilibrium they must), all high-ability workers will prefer the firm that pays $a + q$ because that is where those workers receive the highest earnings. Thus workers who have $q < q^*$ choose to work at firms that pay $a' + bq$, but those firms lose money. All workers who have ability levels greater than q^* choose the firms that pay $a + q$, and those firms break even on the workers. Since breaking even is better than losing, profits are higher for firms that choose the $a + q$ strategy.

As mentioned, many taxicab companies make their drivers full residual claimants after renting the driver the cab. At first glance this arrangement does not seem typical of the standard salesperson's contract. Few salespeople receive 100 percent commission rates. It is more common for firms to pay, say, 10 percent of sales revenue to their salesperson.

The evidence on this point is less clear than it appears. Recall that the worker should be made full residual claimant and that β should be set equal to one. But β multiplies net output, not sales. A residual claimant receives revenues after other variable factors of production have been paid. In the

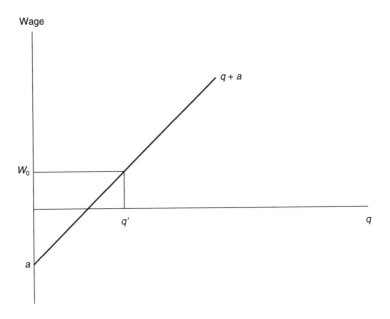

Figure 2.2

case of a computer salesperson, workers who produce the computers and material suppliers must be paid out of revenues. If other costs of production accounted for, say, 80 percent of total revenue, then paying a 20 percent commission rate on sales would be equivalent to paying a 100 percent commission rate on profit as the theory prescribes. So things may not be as far from the risk-neutral model as they first appear.

Another seeming departure from reality is that salespeople generally do not start out with negative earnings. On the contrary, they often receive "draws" or advances against their commissions. Still this is almost identical to the scheme already described where the vertical intercept a is negative. In figure 2.2 the worker receives a draw of W_0, which means that no commissions are paid until q' units are sold. Then the worker receives the standard commission on all units greater than q'. This kinky compensation scheme is nothing more than a spline of a horizontal segment with the line $q + a$. The horizontal segment is only relevant if q falls short of q'. However, in reality, if q falls short of q' repeatedly, the worker loses his job. Thus compensation is dominated by the part of the payment function that is identical to $q + a$.

The amount that a worker is willing to pay for the job (the magnitude of α) depends on the amount of capital with which he works. Drawing on a real world example, Elton (1991) has examined the compensation of American stockbrokers. He found that in large firms with good reputations, the implicit α is more negative than in firms with lesser reputations. This is as it should be. It is easier to sell stock when working for Merrill Lynch than when working for Lazear Securities. Merrill Lynch sets a lower α, consistent with a higher q' for continued employment. It is the constant term, not the slope parameter, that varies across firms.

The firm's CEO has control over the most capital. For this reason standards (the implicit q') are very high. In the case where the CEO is paid $a + q$, the implied value of a is the amount of capital that the CEO rents. In this case it is the entire value of the firm. But it would be impossible to extract such a large payment from an individual. Of course, in equilibrium, no payments must be extracted. The CEO earns a positive salary after having paid the rent, not a negative one. Rather than specifying the formula as explicitly containing a negative intercept term, boards of directors instead give the CEO a fixed wage w_0, as shown in figure 2.2, and set an extremely high q' below which the CEO does not receive any bonus compensation. As long as output is always greater than q', the schemes are equivalent. If output falls below q', the CEO will find that his job is in jeopardy. The implicit q' below which output may not fall without termination is much higher for CEOs than for other workers. As such, the highest-ability workers are selected to be CEOs.

The taxicab example makes clear that setting $\beta = 1$ does not solve all problems. Even if the driver rents the cab and keeps all revenue collected, he still does not have the appropriate incentives to care for capital entrusted to him. Rented cabs tend to be in worse shape than owner-operated cabs. Some have argued that in American football the ability of players to negotiate on their own behalf, independent of their team's interest, has resulted in more injuries. Since team owners cannot capture the full return on the player, teams have less incentive to protect the players' health.[4]

Payment by Input versus Payment by Output

Workers are sometimes paid on the basis of some time unit, such as an hour, day, week, or year, and sometimes on the basis of some measured output, such as the number of pieces of fruit that they pick. How do firms choose between the various compensation methods? If they decide, say, to pay on the basis of output, what formula is used? Salesperson's commission pay, for example, can take many forms and shapes. Which is the equilibrium scheme, and how does it vary with characteristics of the job, industry, or worker? I define a salary as compensation based on input and contrast it with a piece rate, which is compensation based on output. Hourly wages are salaries by this definition because they depend on hours worked—a measure of input—rather than some measure of output. A salary is simply a piece rate with $\beta = 0$ and total salary equal to α as defined in (2.1).

There are a number of factors that affect a firm's choice between payment on input versus payment on output. One important factor is measurement cost. It is often easier to obtain a rough measure of input than it is to obtain an unbiased measure of output. The presence of a worker at his desk signifies some level of input but says nothing about output. The choice between payment on input and payment on output is easily modeled and has some interesting implications.

Let us abstract from effort and suppose that workers have given ability levels that map into a prescribed level of output q. The density of q in the economy is given by $f(q)$ with distribution function $F(q)$. Suppose that workers can work at some alternative job that has a guaranteed wage level of w. Because informational assumptions are crucial here, let us assume that both workers and firms have a symmetric lack of information about worker ability.[5]

A firm can hire workers randomly and simply pay them for showing up at the job. Input-based payment of this kind does not distinguish among workers, whose talents are never measured. Instead, each worker is paid the competitive wage that is equal to a worker's expected output or

$$\text{Salary} = \int_{q_{min}}^{q_{max}} qf(q)\, dq. \tag{2.8}$$

Alternatively, a firm can put a worker on probation for a proportion λ of his work life ($0 \leq \lambda \leq 1$). During that probationary period the worker's output is measured at cost τ, and since his ability is unknown, he is paid expected output. After that time worker output is known, so the worker is paid on the basis of his output.

The advantage of undertaking measurement and paying the corresponding piece rate is that low-quality workers are sorted out to a higher-valued use. Doing so maximizes total output when τ is sufficiently low, and risk-neutral workers prefer this arrangement. Of course, if measurement costs are too high, what is gained by sorting is more than offset by the costs of measurement.

A firm opts to measure workers when the worker's expected pay is higher. Given that the firm has measured the worker's performance, it always pays to use the information in some way. This amounts to paying piece rates that are therefore used when the expected wage at the piece rate firm exceeds that at the salary firm. Since all workers are assumed to be identically ignorant and risk neutral (other assumptions are considered below), they prefer the piece rate scheme when expected lifetime compensation at a piece rate firm exceeds lifetime compensation at a salary firm. Thus they prefer piece rates when

$$\lambda \int_{q_{min}}^{q_{max}} qf(q)\,dq + (1 - \lambda)\left[\int_{w}^{q_{max}} qf(q)\,dq + wF(w)\right] - \tau$$

$$> \int_{q_{min}}^{q_{max}} qf(q)\,dq,$$

or when

$$wF(w) - \int_{q_{min}}^{w} qf(q)\,dq > \frac{\tau}{1 - \lambda}. \tag{2.9}$$

The expression in (2.9) has the following implications:

1. Firms pay on input rather than output when the cost of measurement is high. The inequality favoring piece rates is less likely to hold as τ gets large.

2. Firms pay on input rather than output when measurement requires a long time. It makes no sense to spend valuable resources measuring worker productivity if workers are close to the end of their careers by the time the information has been gathered. In the limit, when $\lambda = 1$, the right-hand side is infinite so a piece rate is never used.

3. The higher the value of the alternative use of time w, the more likely is payment to be output based. Under these circumstances it pays to weed out bad workers because their alternatives are good. Further the higher the alternative wage, the larger the proportion of workers who are better suited to the alternative activity.[6]

4. As a corollary, workers who do not have a great deal of firm-specific human capital are the best candidates for payment on output. If worker productivity at the current firm is much greater than it is elsewhere, worker sorting, which costs τ per worker, is less likely to be worthwhile. Thus young workers with less specific human capital are better candidates for

payment on the basis of output. It makes little sense to measure the output of full professors because they are unlikely to have an alternative at which they are more productive than they are in their current activity.

5. The more heterogeneous the work force, the more valuable is output-based pay. It does not pay to measure the entire work force to weed out workers who are only slightly worse than the average. Sorting is most valuable when there are some workers who are so poorly suited to the firm that they dramatically lower average output. Formally this is captured by the second term on the left-hand side of (2.9). This is the (nonnormalized) expected output among those workers who would leave the firm if payment were based on output. When this term is very low, the left-hand side is high, and thus a piece rate scheme becomes more attractive.

Before leaving this topic, it is useful to consider the role of risk aversion. In the previous example sufficiently risk-averse workers might always prefer the straight salary based on input. While some average income might be sacrificed, the straight salary without measurement provides complete income insurance to the worker. The cost is the difference between the expected lifetime wage under a piece rate and the expected lifetime wage under a salary. Put differently, while firms may be able to smooth income for a given worker over time, major problems arise when firms attempt to insure income across individuals. A worker's output can be low either because he has had bad luck or because he has not put forth sufficient effort. Unless effort is observable, it will be difficult to disentangle the two factors. As a result workers who are insured will have an incentive to shirk and blame their low levels of output on bad luck. In equilibrium everyone shirks, which results in low output and low wages. Thus the "load" that would have to placed on this kind of insurance is likely to be too high to justify much of it in the labor market.

There is evidence on this point. Not only is most of the wage variation across individuals for wage and salary workers, but it also is much larger than the variation for self-employed workers. Since self-employed workers cannot have already entered into insurance contracts as wage and salary workers may have, the wages of the self-employed are a good measure of the independent ability variation component, as it affects output. Since so much variation is present among the self-employed, the a priori evidence against insurance is quite strong.

Others, notably Stiglitz (1975) and Holmstrom (1979), have focused on the trade-off between risk and incentives. The same kind of argument applies. Making workers full residual claimants provides the best incentives when workers are risk neutral. But risk-averse workers object to this kind of compensation scheme, especially when the noise component (v above) accounts for a large part of the variation in output. Not only does a compensation scheme that caters to risk aversion induce moral hazard, it also causes adverse selection, as shown above. Low-quality workers prefer firms with low β and high α, independent of risk considerations. Because moral hazard and adverse selection problems are so pronounced, it is difficult to believe that insurance motives have much of an effect on optimal compensation schemes. Most of the variation in wages is across individuals, not over time, and it is this residual cross-sectional variation that is most difficult to insure without causing other problems.

Payment by output induces workers who are inefficient to leave the firm. If workers are paid exactly their output, they will leave whenever their payments fall short of their alternative wage. But if their payments fall short of their alternative wage, then their output has also fallen short of their marginal product at the other job. As a result all workers who are inefficiently employed at the current firm will quit voluntarily when paid a piece rate. Conversely, all workers whose payments exceed the alternative wage are also those for whom output exceeds their marginal product in the alternative job. They are the workers who efficiency dictates should stay at their current firm.

Besides risk there are other factors that affect the choice between paying a salary and paying a piece rate. Most frequently mentioned is the trade-off between quantity and quality. It is often argued that paying a piece rate induces workers to focus on producing a high number of low-quality units. The quality must of course be sufficiently high so that the output "counts," but the worker, it is alleged, is unconcerned with the unit's quality beyond that.

Piece rates do not necessarily overweight quantity. The exact compensation formula determines the emphasis on the one versus the other. For example, the typist who is paid on the basis of the number of the pages typed goes too quickly and makes too many errors. On the other hand, the typist who is penalized significantly for each error may actually end up typing too slowly and producing too few pages. Thus there is always an appropriate compensation formula that will induce workers to put forth the right amount of effort toward quantity and quality. It should mimic the trade-off between quantity and quality that consumers make in their demand for the final good being produced.

One problem is that quality is often more difficult to observe than quantity. Under these circumstances it is better to pay on the basis of input rather than on the basis of output. A worker who is paid on the basis of his level of effort has no incentive to err in one direction or another with respect to quality versus quantity. Under these circumstances workers can simply be given an instruction as to how much time to devote to each unit. Workers who are paid on the basis of time are, to a first approximation, indifferent between spending a great deal of time producing one unit and spending much less time per unit but producing many more units.

This problem has been modeled explicitly by George Baker (1992), who has analyzed the optimal compensation scheme when output is measured imperfectly. The general result is that the optimal piece rate β moves toward zero as the index of output becomes a poor measure of the true output. As the measure becomes more accurate, the optimal piece rate coefficient moves toward one.

Another problem associated with piece rates is what is commonly called the ratchet effect, which consists of the following problem: Workers who work hard during the first period may signal to the employer that the task is less difficult than anticipated. As a result firms that can lock workers in will attempt to exploit them by lowering the piece rate during subsequent periods. Workers who know this respond optimally by reducing effort in the first period so as not to tip off the employer that work is accomplished so easily. Effort is reduced below the optimal level as an unfortunate consequence of this kind of optimizing behavior.

A judiciously chosen compensation scheme can deal with this problem in a reasonable fashion. Consider the problem in a two-period context. The optimal β exceeds one during the first period in order to offset the tendency of effort to reduce workers below the optimal level. In period 2, β is set equal to one exactly, since there is no subsequent period during which the ratchet effect can operate. As a result workers perform optimally. Each period has its own constant term α to ensure that total compensation over the two periods is just sufficient to attract the worker to the firm and also ensure that workers do not leave after the first period. Piece rates should decline over the work life, but they should start out at a rate greater than one when the ratchet effect is important.[7]

3   Relative Compensation

Piece rates are incentive devices that operate independent of any social environment. Specifically, workers need not be working with anyone else to be motivated by a piece rate scheme. Nor is the presence of other workers even relevant in many contexts. Piece rate compensation is based on an individual's absolute performance rather than his performance relative to some standard or some other individual. But many, including myself, believe that most motivation is produced not by an absolute reward but by compensation that is based on relative comparisons. Specifically, managerial employees who move up the corporate ladder do so by being better than their peers, not necessarily by being good. The same is true of young professors in search of tenure.

Relative versus Absolute

Comparisons are key not only in tenure decisions but also in determining promotions in private enterprise. Since promotions carry with them higher salaries, higher status, and perhaps more interesting assignments, workers seek to get promotions. In the process of doing so, they exert effort in an attempt to outperform their neighbors. Thus relative comparisons can provide as effective incentives as a piece rate or output-based compensation scheme based on individual performance.

Further there are good reasons why firms may prefer to use relative compensation schemes. Two come to mind. The first is that it may be easier to observe relative position than it is to observe absolute position. For example, consider coal mining: Two workers are sent into a mine at the beginning of a day. At the end of the day they bring out their piles of coal. It may be easier to eyeball the two piles and note which one is larger than to determine how much each particular pile of coal weighs in an unbiased way. Second, relative comparisons difference out common noise that risk-averse workers may not like. For example, two salespeople may have a very poor day, not because they did not put forth sufficient effort but because the economy was bad, a condition over which they had no control. If relative compensation is used, the effect of the economy is the same on both individuals and so the individual who performs better will still end up receiving the higher level of compensation.

Relative compensation theory, or "tournament theory" as it has come to be called,[1] is the theory used to determine the size of a raise associated with a particular promotion. It has three essential features. The metaphor of a tennis tournament is useful. Suppose that a Swedish promoter organizes a tennis tournament between Stefan Edberg and Bjorn Borg.

First, note that prizes are fixed in advance and are independent of absolute performance. Suppose that Borg wins the match. He receives a fixed prize that does not depend on the amount by which he beats Edberg. Furthermore both players may do exceedingly well and play an extremely tight contest. The total prize money will not be affected, nor will the distribution of prizes between the individual players be altered.

In the context of the firm this means that there are wage slots that are fixed in advance. There may be one vice-president slot and four assistant vice-president slots. The person who becomes vice-president enjoys the higher wage associated with the vice-president slot. The tournament model, taken literally, implies that the wage that goes to the vice-president is independent of the amount by which he exceeds the performance of the assistant vice-presidents in winning the job.

Second, a player receives the winner's or loser's prize not by being good or bad but by being better than, or worse than, the other player. Again relative performance rather than absolute performance is key. Borg wins the top prize because he is better than Edberg, not because he is good. It is the comparison between the two that is essential. In the context of the corporation, a worker is promoted not because he is good, but because he is better than everybody else in his cohort.

The third feature of relative compensation theory is that the effort with which the worker pursues the promotion depends on the size of the salary increase that comes with the promotion. Suppose that the prize money consists of $500,000. The prizes could be split evenly so that the winner gets $250,000 and the loser gets $250,000. Under these circumstances neither player would be particularly keen on winning and not much effort would be devoted to the activity. If, on the other hand, the winner took $500,000 and the loser took zero, a great deal of effort would be put into the activity. This suggests that the larger the raise associated with the given promotion, the higher the level of effort exerted to win that promotion.

Why then not allow the size of the raise, or the "spread," to go to infinity? After all, it is possible to create any size spread desired simply by requiring workers to ante up some amount initially and then allowing the winner to take everyone's ante in addition to the prize money. For example, suppose that the prize money is $500,000 but that we would like to create a $1 million spread between winner's prize and loser's prize. To do so, simply require that each contestant put up $250,000 going into the contest. The winner takes his own ante of $250,000 back, plus the $500,000 prize money, plus the other player's ante. The loser simply forfeits his $250,000 ante. Thus the loser comes out with −$250,000 and the winner comes out +$750,000, creating a spread of a million dollars. By changing the ante, any spread can be created.

But the optimal amount of effort is not infinite. Even if a principal could dictate the amount of effort that an agent put into a particular project, it would be a finite level because after some point the additional compensation necessary to pay for the additional effort would not be justified by the incremental output associated with that effort.

To make the point vivid, think back to ancient Rome, where the difference between the prize going to the winning gladiator and the prize going to the losing gladiator was about as large as one could imagine. But the problem was that gladiators had to be drafted into service because people did not voluntarily sign up for the job. While the spread was large, the average salary was not sufficient to induce people to risk their lives for the compensation. Given the amount of effort associated with the activity, and the size of the average prize (the prizes were life to the winner and death to the loser), gladiators rarely volunteered for the job. It would be quite possible of course, with the appropriate level of compensation, to induce some people to volunteer. For example, a sufficiently large payment to their heirs could induce some men to compete for their lives. After all, that is exactly what happens when individuals volunteer for military campaigns. While the level of effort is high, and the loser's prize is extremely negative, the gains from winning are sufficiently large to induce people to enlist. This is important because in the context of the firm, individuals must be induced to join the organization voluntarily. Not only must the spread be large to induce effort, but the average prize money must be sufficiently high to attract workers to come to the firm in the first place. Otherwise, workers will opt to enter some other activity.

The mathematics behind this story are quite simple and somewhat illu-
minating. Consider a firm that has only two workers and sets up two jobs:
boss and operator. Workers compete against one another with the winner
being designated boss and the loser being designated operator. The winner receives wage W_1, and the loser receives wage W_2. No wages are paid
until after the contest is completed. The probability of winning the contest
depends on the amount of effort that each individual exerts. Let the two
individuals be denoted j and k and let j's output be given by equation
(3.1a) and k's output by (3.1b).

$$q_j = \mu_j + \varepsilon_j, \tag{3.1a}$$

$$q_k = \mu_k + \varepsilon_k, \tag{3.1b}$$

where μ_j and μ_k are the effort levels of j and k, respectively, ε_j and ε_k are
random luck components, and q_j and q_k are output. The problem can be
split up into two parts. First, worker behavior is modeled. Second, the firm
maximizes profits, taking worker behavior into account by setting up the
optimal compensation scheme.

Equation (3.2) is worker j's optimization problem.

$$\underset{\mu_j}{\text{Max }} W_1 P + W_2(1 - P) - C(\mu_j), \tag{3.2}$$

where W_1 is the boss's wage, W_2 is the worker's wage, and P is the
probability of winning the contest, conditional on the level of effort chosen. Also $C(\mu_j)$ is the monetary value of the pay associated with any given
level of effort μ_j. The first-order condition is

$$(W_1 - W_2)\frac{\partial P}{\partial \mu_j} - C'(\mu_j) = 0. \tag{3.3}$$

There is a corresponding problem for worker k. The probability that j
defeats k is given by

$$P = \text{Prob}(\mu_j + \varepsilon_j > \mu_k + \varepsilon_k) = \text{Prob}(\mu_j - \mu_k > \varepsilon_k - \varepsilon_j)$$

$$= G(\mu_j - \mu_k),$$

where G is the distribution function on the random variable $\varepsilon_k - \varepsilon_j$. Differentiating P with respect to μ_j yields $g(\mu_j - \mu_k)$. Since j and k are ex ante
identical, there should exist a symmetric equilibrium where j and k choose
the same level of effort. Thus at the optimum $\mu_j = \mu_k$, so (3.3) becomes

$$(W_1 - W_2)g(0) = C'(\mu_j). \tag{3.4}$$

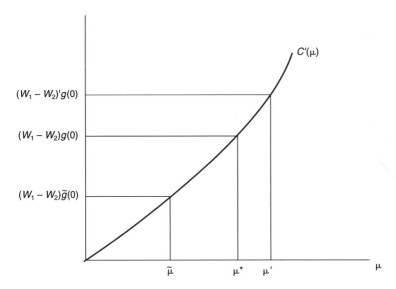

Figure 3.1

Equation (3.4) has two implications that are consistent with the tennis match story. First, the increase in $W_1 - W_2$ implies a higher equilibrium level of effort, since $C'(\mu_j)$ is monotonically increasing in μ. A bigger raise induces workers to compete harder for the promotion.

In figure 3.1, the marginal cost of μ is plotted as $C'(\mu)$. The solution to the first-order condition is where $C'(\mu) = (W_1 - W_2)g(0)$. This implies the solution $\mu = \mu^*$. If the spread were raised to $(W_1 - W_2)'$, the optimum would be at μ' rather than at μ^*. Note that $\mu' > \mu^*$, since $C'(\mu)$ is necessarily increasing in μ.

A second implication is that the lower is $g(0)$, the lower is the level of effort exerted in equilibrium, since $g(0)$ is the measure of the importance of luck in this production environment. When luck is completely unimportant so that $\varepsilon_k - \varepsilon_j$ is degenerate, $g(0)$ goes to infinity. When luck is very important (when the distribution of $\varepsilon_k - \varepsilon_j$ has fat tails), $g(0)$ becomes very small. Thus, as the importance of luck increases, the amount of effort exerted for any given wage spread declines. Again, with reference to figure 3.1, if the spread were $W_1 - W_2$, but the density function were $\tilde{g}(0)$ instead of $g(0)$ (and $\tilde{g}(0) < g(0)$), then the optimum level of μ would be only $\tilde{\mu}$.

The logic behind this result is straightforward. If luck is the dominant factor in determining the outcome of the promotion decision, workers will not try very hard to win the promotion. In production environments where measurements of effort are noisy, large raises must be given in order to offset the tendency by workers to reduce effort. In fact, as will be shown momentarily, it is optimal to offset *any* reduction in effort induced by an increase in the importance of luck.

Let us now turn to the firm's problem. Given the workers' labor supply behavior, characterized by (3.4), the firm now wants to maximize expected profit, or equivalently, profit per worker,[2] since the number of workers hired is exogenous to this problem. The firm's problem then is

$$\underset{W_1, W_2}{\text{Max}} \ \mu - \frac{W_1 + W_2}{2} \tag{3.5}$$

subject to

$$\frac{W_1 + W_2}{2} = C(\mu). \tag{3.6}$$

Equation (3.6) is merely the condition that says that workers must be paid enough, on average, to induce them to apply for the job: $C(\mu)$ is the dollar value of the pain associated with the activity, whereas $(W_1 + W_2)/2$ is the expected wage that each risk-neutral contestant can expect to receive. Condition (3.6) merely says that the expected wage level must be high enough to induce workers to apply. Substituting (3.6) into (3.5) the maximization problem becomes

$$\underset{W_1, W_2}{\text{Max}} \ \mu - C(\mu), \tag{3.7}$$

with first-order conditions

$$\frac{\partial}{\partial W_1} = (1 - C'(\mu)) \frac{\partial \mu}{\partial W_1} = 0,$$

$$\frac{\partial}{\partial W_2} = (1 - C'(\mu)) \frac{\partial \mu}{\partial W_2} = 0. \tag{3.8}$$

The solution to (3.8) implies that $C'(\mu) = 1$. This is the same efficiency condition that appeared in the last chapter of the piece rate problem (see equation (2.7) and recall that μ here is analogous to e in chapter 2). In other words, firms should set up a compensation scheme that induces workers to exert effort up to the point where its marginal cost is equal to its marginal benefit to the firm, namely $1. Thus tournaments are efficient and induce the first-best level of effort. From this relation an optimal level of effort is determined, which after substituting into (3.6) gives the average wage necessary to attract workers to the firm. The wage spread is found by substituting the fact that $C'(\mu) = 1$ into equation (3.4) to obtain

$$W_1 - W_2 = \frac{1}{g(0)}. \tag{3.9}$$

Equations (3.6) and (3.9) are systems of two equations in two unknowns that solve for wage level and wage spread. As promised, the optimal wage spread varies inversely with $g(0)$, so the size of one's wage is increased to offset any increase in luck as reflected by a fall in $g(0)$. Of course the average wage does not change at all as a function of $g(0)$.

American CEOs have recently come under attack for their very high salaries, particularly in comparison to their European and Japanese counterparts. While their salaries may be too high, focusing on their salaries alone misses the entire point of the compensation structure. The CEO's salary is there not so much to motivate the CEO as it is to motivate everyone under him to attempt to attain that job. It is impossible to determine whether the CEO is overpaid simply by looking at the relation of CEO compensation to output. Earlier I argued that the structure of compensation was key; this is what I meant. It makes no sense to evaluate a job independent of the rest of the firm's hierarchical structure.

Tournament theory provides a way to think about the entire structure of compensation within the firm. In this sense it is very different from almost any other theory or set of theories of wages and compensation. Tournament theory implies a particular wage spread, or amount of variance in wages, within an organization. The size of the spread in this simple environment depends exclusively on the amount of noise associated with the production environment. If $g(0)$ is high, reflecting the fact that luck is unimportant in this particular environment, then the wage spread will be small. If $g(0)$ is low, so that luck is extremely important in this production environment, then the wage spread will be large. It is the amount of uncertainty that determines the wage spread and not the absolute output of the CEO.

Many have looked at the ratio of CEO salaries to the average salary of production workers. This is a measure of spread, although perhaps not a perfect one in this environment. But this ratio should depend only on the amount of noise in the environment, and not on the value of the CEO effort. It is misguided to attempt to prescribe some ratio of CEO compensation to production worker salary without understanding the fundamental role of each level's compensation in the entire structure.

The incentive role of salary is particularly important when one compares compensation structures across countries or across industries. Some industries may be riskier than others. The optimality conditions derived above imply that riskier industries should have larger wage spreads than less risky industries in order to induce workers to put forth the appropriate amount of effort. Thus CEOs in firms where demand or cost conditions vary significantly should be very well paid relative to production workers in those industries. In safer industries CEOs should be less well paid relative to production workers. Also note that this result does not depend on the existence of risk aversion. Throughout this chapter I have assumed that workers are risk neutral. It is the incentive aspect of a wage spread that induces high variance in noisy production processes and has nothing to do with distaste for risk.

If Japanese workers produced output in a less risky environment than American workers, then Japanese firms would optimally use a less skewed salary structure than American firms. European firms might find themselves somewhere in the middle. All of these would be optimal and would simply reflect the appropriate compensation structure.

It is important to think in terms of structures to understand compensation at all. For example, many American CEOs receive a large portion of their compensation in the form of stock and stock options. This is a natural response to the inability to use promotion as an incentive device for the top person in the firm. In the absence of relative comparisons, motivation of the top person must be provided through something akin to a piece rate. Stock price can be viewed as a proxy for CEO performance and is a natural instrument for CEO compensation.

Since tournament theory is new, it is difficult to provide specific evidence on the importance of the tournament story. But there are some empirical results. Main, O'Reilly, and Wade (1993) test tournament theory using data from large corporations in examining the relation of CEO compensation to that at the vice-president level. They attempt to find correlations, which they argue should be implications of the tournament model, between these ratios and a number of other factors. They find mild support for tournament theories, but they also argue that some of their results are inconsistent with the theory.

Knoeber (1989) examines compensation of chicken ranchers. He finds they are paid according to a tournament structure, which is a way to difference out common random components (the major one being weather) that affect chicken survival rates. Knoeber finds strong support for tournament theory in his paper and in a subsequent one (Knoeber and Thurman

1994), which also distinguishes between tournament theory and other relative compensation schemes that do not set up specific job slots. The distinction between tournament theory and other relative compensation theories will be discussed in depth in chapter 7.

Ehrenberg and Bognanno (1990) use data from the Professional Golf Association to determine whether prize money and its structure affect scores in golf tournaments. Surprisingly the predictions of tournament theory are borne out very clearly by their data, even in an activity where one would not think effort would be particularly sensitive to incentive pay. The Ehrenberg and Bognanno work is perhaps the best test of tournament theory, not because it is easily generalizable to the corporation but rather because the data are so well suited to testing the model.

Asch (1990) examines the response by navy recruiters to particular prize structures. She finds that they behave as tournament theory would predict and also points to some adverse consequences of prize structure pay. For example, she finds that recruiters substitute effort over time to win prizes and substitute quantity for quality when prizes are specified in terms of relative quantity goals as opposed, say, to more subjective performance evaluations.

Finally, Bull, Schotter, and Weigelt (1987) conduct experiments with college students. They find that the Nash equilibrium predicted by the tournament model is attained very quickly and that the predictions of the tournament model with respect to spread and variance are borne out in classroom experiments.

Industrial Politics

Tournament theory leads directly to a view of industrial politics (see Lazear 1989). Relative comparisons are key in tournament theory and this sets up an environment where competition between workers is likely. Indeed the way by which relative compensation motivates workers is by pitting one against the other, an action that provides incentives to put forth effort. But an adverse consequence of the competition is that workers will not want to cooperate with one another when they feel that they are competing for the same job.

In Lazear (1989) the implications of relative compensation for internal worker interaction are explored. Formally, the industrial politics model is quite similar to the one already presented. The difference is that equations (3.1a) and (3.1b) are changed to

$$q_j = \mu_j - \eta_k + \varepsilon_j,$$

(3.10)

$$q_k = \mu_j - \eta_j + \varepsilon_k,$$

where η_k is the harm k can inflict on j and η_j is the harm that j can inflict on k. In a relative environment, j does well not only by making himself look good but also by making k look bad. While it may be costly to engage in this type of sabotage, it pays for j and k to undertake some of the activity to the extent that it furthers their own relative positions. Workers do not want to cooperate with one another because their compensation depends upon "defeating" other workers within the firm.

Firms that recognize that workers are engaged in sabotage or other uncooperative behavior must adopt policies that mitigate the effects of these actions. Pay compression is a natural outgrowth of this situation. When the difference between the winner's salary and the loser's salary is reduced, two things happen. First, effort falls below the optimal level as workers respond to a smaller spread by decreasing their activities to obtain the promotion. This is bad. Second, workers reduce their anticooperative behavior because winning the contest is less valuable and engaging in sabotage or other adverse activity is costly to the individual who initiates the action. This is good. Thus pay compression, which works in the direction of equality, also enhances efficiency.

Tournament theory, then, implies salary compression, and the implications are very much in line with the standard stories told by personnel managers. Human resources managers often claim that salaries must be compressed to maintain internal harmony in a firm. If the difference between the winner's salary and the loser's salary is too great, morale suffers. One interpretation of the adverse impact on morale is that workers try too hard to disrupt one another's attempts to obtain the coveted position.

Individuals may differ in their ability to engage in sabotage or uncooperative behavior. Some people may be particularly good at attacking others, whereas some individuals may find it extremely costly to engage in this type of activity. Let us label the two types "hawks" and "doves," respectively. Hawks are individuals with an absolute advantage in attacking their neighbors.

Should personality should be a factor in the hiring decision? Intuition goes in both directions. Perhaps putting hawks in with doves makes the normally complacent doves hungrier, implying a positive effect on output. An alternative is that doves who are put in with hawks do not produce at their optimum level because hawks must be controlled by one means or another, and these control mechanisms have adverse effects on the effort level of doves.

The result is that the second argument wins out. If hawks and doves are put together, the optimal compensation strategy is to compress the wage spread to reduce the incentive of hawks to engage in negative activity. This reduces the effort not only of hawks but also of doves. However, if doves can be separated from hawks, the wage spread in a dove's firm can be set at its optimally higher level, implying that dove effort will not suffer. Furthermore the hawks in the firm will also have a compensation system that caters more closely to the direct interests of hawks. Total output is higher when different worker types are sorted into separate firms. Thus segregation rather than integration of worker types is best.

Many firms worry a great deal about their "culture" and whether a new employee fits nicely into it. Resources are devoted to screening an individual not only on the basis of ability level but also on the basis of personality attributes. Yet other firms argue that personality does not matter and that only ability is relevant. Indeed some firms (or academic departments) pride themselves on their willingness to ignore personality and to focus solely on quality. Which type of firm is doing the right thing?

This is simply a question of the existence of a separating equilibrium. Firms need not devote resources to screening workers if workers self-sort. But it can be shown that as a general matter, workers will not self-sort. Under most circumstances hawks will want to pass themselves off as doves for two reasons. First, the output in dovish firms is higher because no sabotage occurs. Second, hawks have an advantage in beating out doves for promotions. As a result firms cannot, as a general matter, afford the luxury of allowing workers to simply self-select.

Of course this does not mean that all firms must invest in screening. A firm that consists solely of hawks need not worry about doves attempting to contaminate the pool. But dovish firms must invest heavily in screening out hawks. I often joke that the University of Chicago, where I've spent most of career, does not screen on the basis of personality because it is already dominated by hawks. Any dove who is interested in coming there is welcome. He raises the output of the firm and is easy game. At less aggressive departments, hawks are discouraged from applying, and personality matters a great deal.

Tournament theory provides some implications for the compensation method appropriate for each level of the hierarchy. It is quite easy to show that individuals who have a comparative advantage in sabotage will be overrepresented in the higher levels of the firm. The reason is straightforward. Individuals can defeat their rivals in corporate challenges either by being able workers or by being good at making their rivals look bad. Unless the two characteristics are sufficiently negatively correlated, individuals who succeed are likely to have a higher than average level of ability and a higher than average level of aggressiveness. As one gets to the very top levels of firms, individuals are extremely able but also extremely aggressive. It is often remarked that CEOs tend to be among the least compassionate people in an organization. Tournament theory suggests that this result follows directly from having to fight the corporate war. Standard Bayesian updating shows that selecting on winning necessarily favors those whose underlying personal characteristics lean toward aggressiveness.

Since the high positions in organizations tend to be dominated by more aggressive individuals, it is necessary to reduce the incentives for those workers to compete with one another. Otherwise, all cooperation will be lost. Compensation at the top of the firm then should be based on absolute performance to a greater extent than compensation for middle-level managers. Since the upper ranks of the organization tend to be dominated by hawks, it pays to sacrifice some effort in order to prevent these extremely competitive individuals from killing each other off.

Another way to reduce the adverse affects of aggressive behavior is to set up the structure of the firm in a way that minimizes the consequences of such behavior. Two real world examples come to mind.

Before the breakup of AT&T, the president of the corporation was generally chosen from among the ranks of the presidents of the subsidiary operating companies. Thus the president of Illinois Bell or Pacific Telephone was more likely to become the president of AT&T than was the executive vice-president at the AT&T corporate office. One reason to select presidents from the field offices is that doing so prevents competition among vice-presidents at the AT&T head office. Competition among these individuals can be extremely destructive to the output of the firm, since their cooperation is highly desirable. While cooperation between the president of Illinois Bell and the president of Pacific Telephone might also be desirable, it is much less important to the output of the firm than is cooperation among individuals at the head office. Thus setting up competitions between individuals at the various subsidiaries who have little contact with one another is a better way to run an organization. It can be quite destructive to have individuals compete with one another when their cooperation is important.

This conclusion leads to a theory of organizational structure because it suggests that it may be better to have individuals compete across product lines than within function lines. More will be said about this in chapter 10.

Another example of how to structure a firm so as to minimize the consequences of aggressive behavior is provided by Dow Chemical Corporation. At Dow, individuals move from field offices to the corporate headquarters in Midland, Michigan. One executive told me that doing this creates a much more cooperative environment in the head office. Each individual knows that he will move into high-level jobs at the head office only after successful completion of fieldwork. This leads to competition among the field offices, but cooperation between field offices is not particularly important for the survival of the organization. On the other hand, cooperation at headquarters is much more important, so movements from the field to headquarters are more frequent than movements from headquarters back out to the field. If competition for the best field jobs occurred at the head office, then managers in Midland, Michigan, would be less cooperative with one another. Thus tournament theory not only provides a basis for thinking about industrial politics but also leads to a theory of hierarchical structure as well.[3]

4   Work-Life Incentive Schemes

How does a firm motivate workers who are locked into a particular position and are virtually certain to remain there without a promotion for the rest of their careers?[1] One way is to make future raises contingent upon current performance. If workers plan to stay with an organization for a significant period of time, then the prospect of receiving a large raise can have important incentive effects, especially if that raise is a permanent one in real terms. Even if a worker's job title does not change, he may still be rewarded in the form of wage growth.

In some respects this kind of incentive scheme is very similar to a piece rate. A worker's performance is observed, and then he is compensated on the basis of that performance. There are two differences.

First, the period over which the evaluation is made is usually longer than is typically the case with piece rate pay. When workers are on a piece rate, they generally receive payment for work done over a very recent interval like a two-week period. When raises are used, the interval is usually much longer, generally a year or perhaps even a number of years. Using an upward-sloping experience-earnings profile is akin to a piece rate where the sample period is very long and observation points are infrequent. Here raises are given for good performance.

The second major difference between upward-sloping experience-earnings profiles and piece rates as motivators is that the worker must continue to be employed in order to reap the benefits of a raise for good performance. With piece rate pay the worker's past performance is rewarded in the form of a lump-sum payment, which is not contingent on future employment. In the case of an upward-sloping experience-earnings profile, the worker must remain with the firm in order to capture the rewards for good performance in the past.

The mechanism as first discussed in Lazear (1979, 1981) motivates workers by paying them less than they are worth when they are young

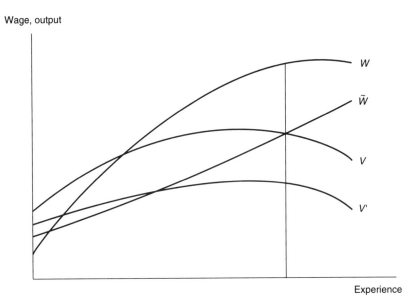

Figure 4.1

and more than they are worth when they are old. This tilted compensation profile is appealing and fits what many personnel managers believe to be occurring within their own organizations. Older workers are paid high salaries, not so much because of superior performance while they are old but rather because their high compensation serves to motivate them during the early years of their careers.

Middle-aged managers are motivated not so much by the hope of future promotions but rather by the hope of raises and continued employment in their current position. Upward-sloping experience-earnings profiles provide these kinds of incentives. An example of this is provided in figure 4.1.

A worker can choose to work at a high level of effort or he may shirk, putting forth a low level of effort. Suppose that a worker's output if he works at a high level of effort is given by the V profile in figure 4.1. If he shirks, his output is V'. But paying the worker V will not provide much of an incentive for him to perform at the high level of output. The $\tilde{W}$ curve in figure 4.1 is the value of the worker's alternative use of time. In this context it is most easily thought of as the value of his leisure. Time T is the date of voluntary and efficient retirement. If workers receive compensation V, they would choose to retire voluntarily at time T because that is the point at which the alternative use of time just equals the worker's marginal product or payment. Any scheme that duplicates the first-best outcome must have, as one of its features, separation of the worker at time T.

Consider two alternative payment schemes. One pays the worker path V throughout his career and the other pays the worker W, which starts below V but eventually rises above V. W is constructed such that the present value of the W path, from 0 to T, equals the present value of the V path from 0 to T. Workers who had access to capital markets would be indifferent between paths W and V if all else were equal. But all else is not equal. Consider a worker who is being paid according to V. As he approaches time T, he must decide whether to put forth the high level of effort or to shirk. As he nears time T, the incentives to shirk become overwhelming. Consider the worker's decision one day before time T. On that day he may either work at the high level of effort or he may shirk. If he shirks, the worst thing that can possibly happen is the worker gets fired. If he gets fired, he does not receive wage V during the next period, but he does get to enjoy the value of his leisure. At time T the value of leisure and V are equal, so the worker loses nothing by shirking, even if he gets fired. Thus there will come a point at which all workers will opt to shirk who are simply paid their marginal product.

Alternatively, the worker can be paid according to W. Now consider the worker's decision one day before time T. If the worker shirks and is dismissed, he gets to enjoy the value of his leisure $\bar{W}$ next period, but he forgoes wage W. Since W is set such that it is well above V at time T, a worker will forfeit quasi-rents by shirking. Thus the W profile if sufficiently steep will induce workers to perform at a higher level of effort than will the V profile. In fact it would be impossible to pay workers along the V profile because at some point in the worker's career his output would switch to V'.

The steeper age-experience profile W induces workers to put forth high levels of effort for which they receive additional compensation. If workers were paid according to V, they would be induced to put forth lower levels of effort and the entire experience-earnings profile would have to be adjusted downward to take into account this lower productivity. Because firms are limited in their ability to extract penalty payments from workers, forcing workers to forgo higher-than-alternative salaries when they lose their jobs provides an incentive against shirking and malfeasance.

One by-product of this particular compensation scheme is the need for mandatory retirement. Since the wage path W lies above the wage path

$\tilde{W}$, workers will not choose to retire voluntarily at time T. Instead they would prefer to continue working as long as the firm were willing to offer wage W. But doing so would not only bankrupt the firm, it would induce workers to remain with the firm inefficiently long. Mandatory retirement is a consequence of using a profile that pays workers more than their worth at their retirement age.

While this theory was first put forth as an explanation of mandatory retirement, the principle is much more general. The argument here relates more to incentives than it does to mandatory retirement, and this kind of a scheme could be used even in the absence of mandatory retirement. In fact there are alternative institutions that can actually act as well as or better than mandatory retirement to ensure that efficient separation occurs in the firm. Pensions (see Lazear 1982), whose value varies with age of retirement, can be used as a device to buy workers out of their current contracts. These efficient pension schemes, discussed below, accomplish the same goal as mandatory retirement and sometimes do it better.

I believe that this view of life-cycle earnings corresponds quite closely to that held by personnel managers. Senior workers are paid high salaries in the firm not so much for their current productivity but as a reward for past productivity and as a motivator for current productivity of their more junior counterparts.

There has been empirical work to support the contentions of this theory. A number of papers by Hutchens (e.g., 1987, 1989) support the view that upward-sloping age-earnings profiles are used as a motivator when workers are engaged in tasks that produce output that is difficult to observe or measure. Goldin (1986) finds that women are more likely than men to be paid a piece rate historically. She argues that women have less permanent attachments to the work force, so upward-sloping experience-earnings profiles cannot be used as effectively for women. Firms pay women piece rates as an alternative, despite the higher measurement costs. Finally, Kotlikoff (1988) finds evidence based on earnings functions across different occupational categories that is consistent with the life-cycle incentives view.

Pensions

Sometimes a pension can act as a buyout and can induce workers to retire voluntarily at the optimum age. Firms often use explicit pension buyout schemes when special circumstances arise. For example, a firm that would like to undertake a major reduction in force will often offer workers, within

EPV of pension benefits

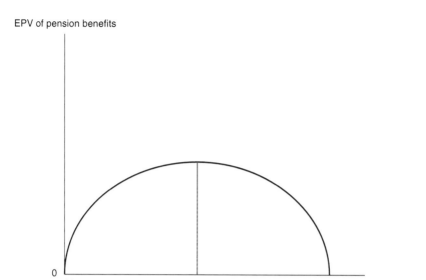

Figure 4.2

a specific age window, the option to leave with a somewhat sweetened pension plan. But independent of explicit pension buyout schemes, or other buyout schemes, the standard defined-benefit pension formula has implicit in it incentives to induce workers to retire. This point is discussed in Lazear (1982, 1983).

The idea is easily seen in the following example: Defined-benefit pension plans generally reward workers for years of service in the form of a higher annual pension during each year of retirement. But the value of that reward declines as the worker lengthens his career. In fact the relation of the expected present value of pension benefits to age of retirement in a typical firm is shown in figure 4.2.

If a worker retires when he is very young, he is not accumulating any pension benefits, so the expected present value of the benefits is zero. At the other extreme, if a worker retires on the day he dies, the annual pension that he should receive is quite high, but since he dies at that point he receives no pension. Thus retiring early or retiring late gives the worker zero pension. Retiring at some intermediate age will give the worker a higher expected present value of pension benefits.

As an empirical matter, the peak of the expected present value of pension benefits in most large corporations occurs at some age between 55 and 65. This means that workers who continue to work beyond this peak age sacrifice pension benefits for each additional year that they work. While they continue to earn their wage rate, the total value of the year's compensation must take into account the decline in pension value. Thus a worker whose salary is constant, in real terms, during the last ten years of his work life is actually receiving a different amount of total compensation in each year. His total compensation depends on where he is in the pension profile. All workers who are younger than T^* in figure 4.2 are being paid more than their current wage, whereas all workers who are older than T^* in the figure are being paid less than their current wage. Depending on the rate of decline in the function shown in figure 4.2, workers may be sacrificing a great deal to continue to work at the job. This is an alternative way to lower wages over a worker's life without having to do so explicitly. In the United States it is perfectly legal and customary to do this, but to do so only implicitly.

There is actually a buyout scheme that, even without mandatory retirement, induces workers to leave voluntarily whenever it is efficient to do so. It is optimal for the worker to leave whenever his alternative use of time exceeds his value at the firm. Suppose that because of fixed costs of hiring, and so forth, a worker cannot leave and return later. Suppose further that a worker receives an unanticipated wage offer $W^*(\tau)$ at some time τ. For efficiency, the worker should leave if

$$e^{r\tau} \int_\tau^T W^*(\tau) e^{-r\tau} d\tau > e^{r\tau} \int_\tau^T V(\tau) e^{-r\tau} d\tau, \tag{4.1}$$

where $V(\tau)$ is his value to the firm at time τ. But the worker leaves voluntarily if and only if

$$e^{r\tau} \int_\tau^T W^*(\tau) e^{-r\tau} d\tau > e^{r\tau} \int_\tau^T W(\tau) e^{-r\tau} d\tau, \tag{4.2}$$

where $W(\tau)$ is his wage at time τ if he stays with the firm. Let the firm offer a buyout, $S(\tau)$, where

$$S(\tau) \equiv e^{r\tau} \int_\tau^T [W(t) - V(t)] e^{-r\tau} d\tau. \tag{4.3}$$

Note that as $\tau \to T$, $S(\tau)$ approaches zero. The efficient severance pay at T equals zero.

Now the worker's decision is modified. Instead of leaving whenever (4.2) holds, he leaves iff

$$e^{r\tau} \int_\tau^T W^*(\tau)e^{r\tau}\,d\tau + S(\tau) > e^{r\tau} \int_\tau^T W(\tau)e^{-r\tau}\,d\tau. \qquad (4.4)$$

Substituting (4.3) into (4.4) yields that the worker leaves iff

$$e^{r\tau} \int_\tau^T [W^*(\tau) - V(\tau)]e^{-r\tau}\,d\tau > 0, \qquad (4.5)$$

which is the same condition as (4.1). Thus offering severance pay $S(\tau)$ as defined in (4.3) induces the worker to leave when it is efficient to do so.

As already mentioned, $S(\tau)$ goes to zero at T. If $S(\tau)$ is defined as in (4.3), then its typical pattern will have the shape shown in figure 4.2; that is, $S(\tau)$ will start out small, rise to some peak, and then decline as the worker reaches the appropriate age of retirement.

As already mentioned, in examining two data sets coming from similar samples in two different years, I have found that the pattern of the expected present value of pensions resembles that which would be predicted by equation (4.3). Not only is the shape correct, but the numbers seem to be of the appropriate magnitudes to induce workers to retire efficiently. This is quite a remarkable finding; there is nothing that automatically links the expected present value of pension payments and its decline with additional years of the work life to $S(\tau)$, which is the difference between wages and the worker's marginal product. These pieces of independent evidence suggest two things. First, upward-sloping age-earnings profiles are indeed used as a motivating device, and second, blunt instruments, such as mandatory retirement, can be replaced by more refined ones, such as efficient pension plans, to induce workers to exhibit efficient labor supply behavior.

Team Compensation

If variable pay is the buzzword of personnel, the mere mention of teams and team compensation can make a human resources manager quiver with emotion. In large part the interest in team compensation has been generated by the success of the Japanese who seem to use team production to a greater extent than firms throughout Europe and the United States. Further the academic industrial psychologists and sociologists who study these issues have jumped on the bandwagon. Many argue that group incentives can be a more effective motivator under certain circumstances than can individual incentive schemes. Most of the discussion on these points has been loose, and the somewhat unspecific nature of the argument has led to more confusion than clarity.

Free-Rider Problems and Compensation Method

Kandel and Lazear (1992) attempt to examine the role of team incentives in a more rigorous fashion. It is difficult to understand why team compensation can be an effective motivator in anything but a very small team. For example, Japanese firms, where profit sharing supposedly counts for a large component of compensation, have an extremely large number of workers. An additional dollar of output, when divided among the many workers in the organization, contributes only a trivial amount to any individual worker's compensation. Furthermore the output of any small group contributes only a trivial amount to the compensation of members of that group. Thus there is no clear reason why one team should not simply shirk and free ride on all the other teams in the organization.[1]

Incentives are probably not at the heart of compensation in a Japanese organization, although there may be some incentive considerations at work. An alternative interpretation is that the profit sharing is simply a way to distribute risk to Japanese workers who do not hold a large amount of private securities. If Japanese workers are essentially equity holders in their organizations through their wages, and if their organizations invest and hold securities in other corporations within the economy, then the firm acts as a financial intermediary to perform a financial market-smoothing process. Rather than taking pecuniary compensation from the organizations and then investing privately in financial markets, workers simply forgo wages. Their firms then use the revenues generated by these forgone earnings and invest them in the securities of other organizations. The returns and dividends from those securities accrue to the workers' firm and are passed along later in life in the form of higher wages. To the extent that the wages Japanese workers receive are contingent upon the overall profitability of the firm (which depends on the returns to other corporations' stock), workers are implicit equity holders in the firm.[2]

Still, many observers believe that the attitudes and work ethic of organizations where profit sharing is important are very different from the attitudes and work ethic in firms whose compensation is strictly wage and salary, without any significant profit-sharing component. Kandel and Lazear (1992) distinguish between shame and guilt, terms used by sociologists to describe individuals in relation to their peers and societies at large. Sociologists have used the terms shame and guilt to contrast societies that are motivated by internal pressure with those that are motivated by external pressure. Shame-based societies are those where peer pressure comes directly from others as a response to some action that works to the detriment of the group as a whole. In guilt-based societies, individuals are motivated to do well not so much by the direct pressure of their peers but by feelings internalized toward their comrades. Thus in a guilt-oriented society the worker is reluctant to shirk because doing so brings on bad feelings about what he is doing to others. Our interpretation is that sociologists use shame to denote peer pressure when output or effort is observable. Guilt, on the other hand, works even when neither effort nor individual output can be observed, since guilt is internalized. Thus organizations may try to instill guilt in their workers, euphemistically called loyalty, in their attempt to encourage performance in environments where others cannot observe the shirking.

A classic example comes from the military. Soldiers are run through an extensive boot camp training program that makes soldiers loyal to one another and creates, in their consciences, an awareness of a common enemy. Much of the training acquired during boot camp is useless to the typical soldier, who may end up being a supply clerk stationed in North Carolina. Still the military spends a great deal of time and money on building bonds between soldiers so that these bonds may later be an effective motivator in rare circumstances that have extreme importance. For example, a soldier out on a scouting mission alone is in great danger. It would be rational to lie low, hide, and stay out of trouble. Instead, scouts often undertake significant risk in order to protect their platoon mates. They feel loyalty to their fellow soldiers, which causes them to take actions that would otherwise not be in their self interest. Letting their peers down would instill guilt, which is a useful motivator in this situation where their actions are not easily monitored.

A necessary ingredient is some sort of profit sharing. If workers do not share in the profits of the enterprise but rather are paid a straight salary, then shirking by one worker in no way affects the utility of his peers. When workers are not residual claimants, loyalty to other workers will not motivate an individual to put forth additional effort. In the case of the military example above, soldiers are "profit sharers." Actions by one soldier have direct implications for the happiness of other soldiers. Similarly peer pressure, the effectiveness of guilt, shame, and other forms of implicit motivation are tied directly to profit sharing. Thus organizations that invest heavily in creating bonds between workers are those that also should have a high degree of profit sharing.

The point is less obvious than it seems, however. When a worker shirks, he necessarily affects someone else's utility. In the case where workers are paid a straight salary, capital is adversely affected by workers' shirking. When workers are profit sharers, then other workers as well as capital owners are affected. But it is not obvious that workers should care more about harming other workers than they do about harming capital owners. To make the case that profit sharing has incentive effects, it is necessary to argue that workers empathize more with their fellow workers than they do with faceless shareholders. Such arguments are not implausible, but they are a necessary component of any case to be made for profit sharing within an organization. If workers empathize with nonlabor capital owners as much as they do with other workers, then there will be no gains to using a profit-sharing scheme. The free-rider effect is simply too significant to imply much motivation on the basis of individual compensation. It is only when others are affected, and those others are individuals about whom the specific worker cares, that profit sharing can act as a motivating force.

The notions of loyalty, guilt, and shame can be parameterized and dealt with rigorously in a theoretical framework. Doing so assists in the understanding of what the sociologists term "norm." Norms can be thought of

more rigorously as the equilibrium level of effort that results when an
organization punishes deviance. The larger the punishment for deviating
from the norm, the higher will be the equilibrium level established as the
norm in the firm. Personnel managers who understand how norms are
established can then implement higher levels of effort as the norm level
simply by creating larger punishments for falling short of the norm.

For example, let the worker's utility function be given by

$$u = \frac{Q}{N} - c(e) - \lambda(\bar{e} - e),$$

where Q is total output of the firm, e is the individual's effort, $c(e)$ is the
pain associated with effort, and $\bar{e}$ is the average effort level of the worker's
peers. The last term, parameterized by λ (and independent of N), reflects
guilt or shame.

The first-order condition is

$$\frac{\partial Q/\partial e}{N} + \lambda = c'(e).$$

Since $c'(e)$ is increasing in effort, the larger the λ, the larger is the chosen
level of effort. In the simplest case, where all workers are identical, $\bar{e} = e$
and is determined by the foc above. Further the higher the λ, the higher
will be the "norm" level of effort in the firm. Thus establishing a higher
norm level of effort requires that the penalty, associated with negative
deviations from the norm, rise.

The work by Kandel and myself contrasts somewhat with the earlier
work by Holmstrom (1982). Holmstrom focuses on work sharing as a way
to motivate workers. He analyzes the so-called Stalin schemes, which assign a task to a team of workers and then punish all members for failure to
complete the task. In this environment, shirking must be made up for by
another worker's increased effort. Peer pressure may be an effective way to
induce workers to carry their own weight. But gang behavior and other
bullying kinds of activities can prevent this scheme from being an effective
one. A group of buddies may shirk. Others must make up for their reduced
effort if the buddies cannot be forced by their peers to work. Additionally
the focus of Holmstrom's work is on mechanisms that require a third party.
Many problems involving profit sharing do not necessitate a third party.
Indeed the essence of a partnership is that third parties are not included in
the agreement. Partners must structure an incentive scheme that induces all
individuals to work in the absence of an outside enforcer.

Some empirical evidence on the importance of profit sharing and partnership in professional practices is provided by Gilson and Mnookin (1985), who explore compensation and profit sharing in law firms. They find that compensation is not the same across partners but that compensation differs to a lesser extent than contribution to the firm as measured by observables. "Rainmakers" do earn higher salaries than other attorneys in the firm, but their reward is in no way proportional to the amount of business they generate. In part, this can be explained by complementarities within the firm. Rainmakers can generate business only to the extent that other attorneys are producing high-quality output, so attributing all the business to the individual who actually brings it in is probably inappropriate. Still, rationalizations of this sort can only go part of the way toward explaining the wage compression. Thus profit sharing is a significant part of compensation in law firms.

Gaynor and Pauly (1990) examined incentives in medical practices. They argue that incentives are diluted and find that productivity is reduced as the size of the medical practice increases. Whether these differences reflect selection or moral hazard is, of course, difficult to ascertain, but the findings do conform with the theory. Also Benelli, Loderer, and Lys (1987) examine data from large corporations and find that explicit worker participation in firm decisions has little, if any, effect on corporate operations and performance. Similar findings were obtained by Katz, Keefe, and Kochan (1987), who examined productivity among General Motors plants. They found that in those plants where "new industrial relations" practices were used, output was not higher, and in some instances was lower, than output in traditionally run firms. Selection problems are paramount, but the data on profit sharing and worker participation do not give overwhelming support to the view that worker cooperation has dramatic effects on productivity.

In a somewhat different vein Farrell and Scotchmer (1988) have examined partnerships and obtain a result that appears in a somewhat different context in the literature on worker-run firms. An equal-sharing rule inefficiently limits the size of partnerships because workers care about average product rather than marginal product in an organization. If workers were free to sell the rights to their jobs, however, this result would vanish. Adding positions to the firm is always profitable when the additional positions bring about efficiency. As long as the initial partners could capture the returns to selling those additional positions, partnerships would behave in the same way as a competitive firm.

Stock Incentive Plans

One form of profit sharing makes managers explicit equity holders in the firm. Stock and stock options are sometimes used as compensation devices, often with the term "incentive" attached to them. Whether or not they function as incentive devices remains to be seen. There are a few issues involved, some of which have already come up in the context of profit sharing.

First, suppose that changes in the stock price do reflect changes in the value of the firm and that the market functions close to the efficient market's paradigm If the market perfectly reflected changes in the value of the firm, then output of even the lowliest worker would be fully reflected in the change in stock price (as long as the worker's wage itself were not contingent on output). Even under these circumstances the free-rider problem remains, since each worker receives only a trivial fraction of the amount by which his firm increases effort.

Consider a janitor who improves the output of the firm by one dollar. The janitor is very unlikely to own a large part of the firm's stock and so receives only a trivial portion of that one dollar he produces. As such, the janitor has virtually no incentives to put forth effort. For stock to be a significant motivator, a risk-neutral worker must own a relatively large share of the company.

An additional issue arises. To the extent that compensation already reflects changes in the output of the firm, then none of that change in output shows up in the stock price. Consider, for example, a CEO who is effective in raising the value of the firm by 1 percent. If that CEO's salary goes up, say, through a bonus, by 1 percent of the firm, then residual capital will enjoy no increase in the value of the stock. Specifically this means that if a manager is already being paid a strict piece rate in some form, stock price will not reflect any changes in the output in the firm that result from managerial effort. Those changes will be fully captured by the manager himself, and not by (other) owners of capital.

Let us beg these questions for the time being and ask whether there is a way to think about the incentives inherent in any stock or stock option formula.[3] Consider a firm that is normalized to be worth zero at the outset. Its value next period is given by

$$V = e + v, \tag{5.1}$$

where e is the level of effort chosen by the manager and v is the random component over which the manager has no control. Let the manager be given γ of the firm in stock or stock options. A stock option has an exercise price K and is "in the money" whenever V exceeds K. When $V > K$, it pays the manager to exercise his option and buy the stock at K, reselling at V with a $V - K$ profit. Let the random variable v have density function $f(v)$. Let the cost associated with exerting effort be $C(e)$. The expected value of options to a risk-neutral manager that entitles the manager to buy γ of the firm is

$$Z = \gamma \int_{K-e}^{\infty} (e + v - K)f(v)\,dv,$$

where Z is the expected value of the option.

The manager's problem is to choose effort to maximize

$$\gamma \int_{K-e}^{\infty} (e + v - K)f(v)\,dv - C(e). \tag{5.2}$$

The first-order condition is

$$\gamma[1 - F(K - e)] = C'(e), \tag{5.3}$$

where F is the cumulative distribution function of v.

Inspection of the formula for Z and the first-order condition (5.3) reveals that the trade-off between γ and K in Z is not the same as the trade-off between γ and K in affecting effort. While there are an infinite number of ways to produce a given expected value of option, they do not all provide the same incentives for effort, even for risk-neutral managers. In other words, the left-hand side of (5.3) cannot be rewritten only in terms of Z. Holding Z constant is not sufficient to hold effort constant.

A general result is that with risk neutrality, straight stock should be given. Specifically the strike price should be set sufficiently low so that the option is always in the money. But the same argument does not apply when workers are risk averse. Options that are not always in the money generally are preferred when workers are risk averse. The reason relates back to a point made by Bergson (1978) in the context of command economies. Workers are risk averse. As they become richer, they must be given even higher levels of compensation to induce a particular level of effort. Thus the payoff function needs to be convex. Using options that are not always in the money creates a convex payoff function. When output reaches a sufficiently high level, the option kicks in, creating a discontinuity which is the discrete analogue of convexity in this context.

There are other reasons why risk-averse managers need to be given options that are sometimes out of the money. Project choice has not been variable so far. In the real world managers can of course choose the kinds of projects that they engage in and risk-averse managers tend to choose safer projects over risky ones. In part, this is a function of the manager's employment security. To the extent that managers earn rents on their current jobs, they prefer to keep their jobs, even at a somewhat reduced wage rate. To offset this tendency, options with high strike prices can be used. It is well known that the value of an option increases in the variance of the underlying process. Giving managers options with a positive strike price increases the incentive to undertake risky projects.[4] After all, only a risky project has a significant probability that a high strike price will be exceeded, so managers engage in those projects in order to capture the returns. This means that options with high strike prices induce the managers to behave in a somewhat less risk-averse fashion, which may bring their incentives more into line with shareholders' interest.

A related point explains why managers are always at the long end of a call option, rather than at the short end of put options. An alternative way to motivate a manager is simply to pay him to be short on a put option. If things go badly at the firm, the stock price falls and owners can exercise their right to put the shares to the manager. The manager is then forced to buy the shares at a price above the market price. The manager then assumes some of the shareholders' losses. This provides the same kind of incentive as a call option does. But there is a difference, which relates again to project choice. In the case where the manager is at the short end of the put option, the manager would like to make sure that the variance in the underlying process is low. Managers who are short on puts get hurt badly by very negative outcomes. Thus making a manager short on a put option, while providing incentives to increase the firm's market value, provides incentives for the manager to undertake safe rather than risky projects, thus maintaining the status quo. Again, to the extent that managers already choose projects that are too safe relative to shareholders' desires, it is undesirable to reinforce that tendency.

One point goes in the opposite direction. Usually managers are given options that they can exercise at some date in the relatively far-off future. When the strike price is set too high, the option loses its motivating properties if the stock price falls dramatically during the period. Since stock prices depend on some factors over which a particular manager has no control, stock prices that fall greatly as a result of these other factors are likely to be in the money. If that likelihood falls sufficiently, the manager essentially gives up. He views the likelihood of being in the money as so low that there is little effect of his own effort on changing that probability.

As a result the option loses its incentive properties. On the other hand, if the manager owns stock (an option that is always in the money), the current level of the stock price has no effect on the manager's incentives. Every change in the stock price is captured by the manager fully and is not filtered through a discontinuous process. So, while giving straight stock may have a negative effect on project choice, it has positive effects in terms of the dynamic properties of effort. Formally, examining $\partial e/\partial K|_{(5.3)}$, we find that

$$\frac{\partial e}{\partial K}\Big|_{(5.3)} = \frac{-\gamma f(K - e)}{c'' - f(K - e)}.$$

For large K, $f(K - e)$ gets arbitrarily small so that $c'' - f > 0$, which means that effort declines in K beyond some point.

Free-rider effects can be offset to some extent by choosing a stock option with a high strike price. Suppose that stock is given to a CEO. Even the CEO owns only a small portion of the firm, which means that she captures only a small portion of the return to her effort. To offset this effect, it possible to offer a large number of options with a high strike price in lieu of a smaller number with lower strike prices. This essentially levers the upside that the CEO faces, thereby offsetting her tendency to ignore a large part of the return.

Consider the following example: Suppose that there are two possibilities for ε: good luck, in which case, $v = 1$, or bad luck, in which case $v = -1$. Suppose that the firm were worth $10 initially. Then stock would be priced at $10, reflecting that half of the time, the firm's value would be $11 and half of the time it would be $9. How much would an option with a strike price of $10.50 be worth? The answer is $.25 because the option is in the money half of the time, and when it is in the money, it returns $11 − 10.50 or $.50. Thus, to give a CEO the equivalent of 1 share of stock, she would have to be given 40 options at a strike price of $10.50.

Now suppose that she raises the value of the firm by one dollar. If she owns one share of stock, the return to her one share is $1 divided by the number of shares outstanding in the firm. Suppose that there are 100 shares of stock in the firm altogether. Then her return to raising the value of the firm by $1 is only 1 cent because the value of each share rises to $10.01. The CEO will put forth the effort only it the cost of her effort is less than 1 cent. Say that, instead, she had been given 40 options with a strike price of $10.50. The firm provides shares by buying them from other shareholders at the market price. Initially this has value equivalent to that of the one share of stock. If she raises the value of the firm by $1, then her option will still be in the money only half of the time because the shares will either be worth $9.01 or $11.01 rather than $9 or $11. But when it is in the money, she makes $11.01 − $10.50 per option. So she makes $.51 × 40 one-half of the time rather than only $.50 one-half of the time. Clearly the value of increasing the firm by one dollar is that it changes her expected take by

$$(\tfrac{1}{2}) \times (\$.51 - \$.50) \times 40 = \$.20.$$

Now the CEO will be willing to raise the value of the firm by $1 as long as the cost of her effort is less than $.20 instead of the $.01 in the case of stock. Options provide leverage and allow her to capture more of the return to effort without bearing the downside. As such, options may be a way to offset the free-rider effects inherent in a publicly held company where the CEO cannot own the full amount of the firm because of the stakes involved.

This section began by arguing that stocks and stock options are unlikely to have much of an incentive effect because they are claims to only a very small portion of the firm. While that statement is true, it does not negate the relevance of the previous analysis. Compensation schemes such as bonuses are analogous to stock options when bonuses are tied to some measure of an individual's effort or output and not to aggregate output of the firm. Bonuses, like stock options, can be discontinuous. For example, a manager may be given nothing unless his measured output exceeds some level Q^* and then could be linear in all output above Q^*. Under these circumstances it would have the same properties as the option described above for incentives, but the free-rider effects would not come into play. Such a scheme has already been discussed in the context of piece rates with draws. Figure 2.2 is essentially an option payoff function. The worker receives the constant amount W_0 until Q^* is hit, and then receives an amount linear in Q after Q^*. Such a payoff scheme, which mimics an option, induces managers to take on riskier projects and also induces risk-averse managers to perform at higher levels of effort. All of the results of the last few pages can be generalized to compensation schemes that depend not on some measure of firm output but rather on some measure of individual output, which eliminates any free-rider considerations.

6   Other Issues in Compensation

Nonpecuniary Compensation

Economists are often accused by sociologists and industrial psychologists of being too narrow, in their focusing exclusively on monetary variables and ignoring the perhaps more important psychological ones. As a practical matter, the accusation may be valid in part. But economic theory deals with nonpecuniary attributes of compensation quite easily.

The idea that nonmonetary variables affect the value of a job goes back to Adam Smith (1776). More recently the ideas have been formalized by Rosen (1974). The primary goal of the work done on equalizing differences, or "compensating differentials" as it has come to be called in the literature, is to transform nonpecuniary components of the job into their monetary equivalents. A large number of compensation consultants have used this approach to evaluate jobs on the basis of their skill requirements and nonpecuniary characteristics. Indexes are then derived and are used by firms to set wages for various types of workers. The approach is widespread, but it does have some basic difficulties.

The fundamental identification problem, as discussed by Rosen (1974), can be seen in the following example: As labor force participation rates of women have risen, it has become more common to provide jobs that have more flexible work hours. Let us suppose that there are two types of workers, men and women. Both prefer flexible hours, but women have a stronger preference for flexible hours than men do. Both also like higher wages. The indifference curves are shown in figure 6.1. The dotted indifference curves express the preferences of women, and the solid indifference curves express the preferences of men. There are also two isoprofit contours in the diagram corresponding to firms with two different technologies. The isoprofit curve with the short dashes that goes through point F corresponds to a firm that has a comparative advantage in providing more

Wage

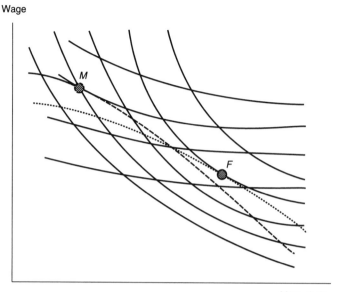

More choice over hours

Figure 6.1

flexible hours. The one with an isoprofit function going through point M corresponds to a firm with a comparative advantage in paying higher wages. Equilibrium is characterized by men choosing to work at the high-wage, inflexible firm and women choosing to work at the low-wage, more flexible firm. Firms of the two types coexist in the same market because each isoprofit curve corresponds to zero profit, so no one firm type is doing any better than the other firm type. There is no incentive to switch from one firm technology to another firm technology.

This is indeed an equilibrium, since there is no way for the flexible firm to offer any package to males that makes them better off than they are at point M that is consistent with nonnegative profit. Similarly there is no way for the high-wage firm to offer a package to females that makes them better off than they are at F that is consistent with nonnegative profits.

Many compensation consulting firms are in the business of estimating market relations between wages and job attributes. They gather data, in this case on wages and flexibility, and end up with a scatter, which in this example, would look like figure 6.2a. Firms would be located either at point M or at point F. A compensation consultant would run a regression of wages on choice over hours, ending up with a line that runs through point M and F, with equation

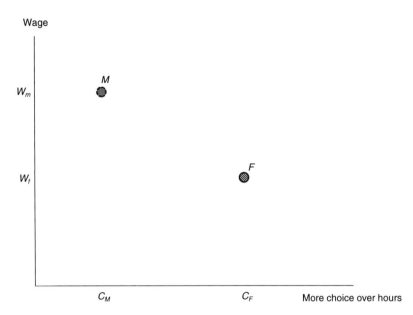

Figure 6.2a

$$\text{Wage} = a + b(\text{choice}). \tag{6.1}$$

Coefficient b, which is obtained from the regression, reflects the market value of an additional unit of hours flexibility. If a firm is willing to increase the amount of choice over hours from C_m to C_f, it can reduce wages from W_m to W_f. But figure 6.1 tells us that the line that goes through points M and F is not an approximation to indifference curves for either men or women. In fact, if the males' firm were to increase flexibility to C_f and reduce wages to W_f, the men at the firm would end up leaving and would have to be replaced by new hires, all of them women. All men would prefer to work at other high wage, low-flexibility firms. Conversely, if a female firm decided to reduce its flexibility from C_f to C_m, but increased wages from W_f to W_m, all women would resign and would have to be replaced by men.

Whether replacement of workers is costly depends on the amount of firm-specific human capital held by the typical worker. If all human capital were general, then separation of the existing work force and replacement by new workers imposes no cost on firms or workers. But when firms and workers have invested in a substantial amount of firm-specific human capital, separation, which destroys the value of the specific human capital, is necessarily costly, both socially and privately. Because workers have sorted according to their tastes, changing both wages and flexibility of hours along the market line will not be acceptable to the current group of workers. In figure 6.1 the regression line that would be observed using market data simply connects points M and F. The slope of that line suggests a trade-off between wages and choice over hours that is too steep for males and too flat for females. A male-dominated firm that attempts to reduce wages and increase hours flexibility in accordance with the market regression line will find its workers unwilling to buy the additional hours flexibility at such a high price as wage reduction. All those males will leave in favor of firms that offer the combination at point M. Conversely, female-dominated firms that attempt to reduce hours flexibility by raising wages in accordance with the market regression line will find their female employees unwilling to accept such a large reduction in hours flexibility for such a relatively small increase in wages. Those women will also leave their firms in favor of another firm that offers the combination at F. Firms that take the advice of compensation consultants on this matter will find their profits fall as they lose the benefit of the firm-specific human capital embedded in their current work force.

In general, the market regression line tells a firm only about its workers' preferences for very small changes. But most personnel policies involve large changes. Because workers sort in accordance with their tastes, the information provided by the compensation consultant will always give a biased picture. Specifically in this context the market regression line always overstates the amount by which wages can be reduced with increased hours flexibility and always understates the amount by which wages must be increased corresponding to a reduction in hours flexibility. Firms that are already paying high wages with less flexible hours have a labor force that has a relative preference for high-wage, less flexible jobs. Firms that are paying low wages and providing more flexible hours employ a work force that has a relative preference for low-wage, flexible jobs. The market line tells us the preference of neither group but rather the locus of trade-offs that can be accomplished by choosing different workers with different preferences.

As a practical matter, b in equation (6.1) is often positive rather than negative, which contradicts the fundamental implication of the compensating differential model. Instead, workers who earn high wages also tend to have high levels of fringe benefits. The failure to find a trade-off between wages and fringes reflects unobserved ability bias. High-ability workers take some of their additional compensation in the form of higher

Wage

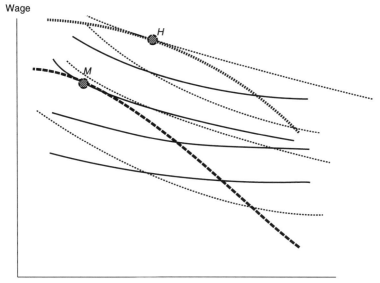

More choice over hours

Figure 6.2b

wages and some of their compensation in the form of more fringes. Since ability is difficult to measure, most of the variation across firms may reflect unobserved worker ability differences rather than a trade-off in ability for a given worker. While the theory still holds, because of ability sorting, it is difficult to pick up the trade-off between wages and fringes independent of ability.

Instead of the data looking as they do in figure 6.1a, they are more likely to appear as they do in figure 6.2b. In figure 6.2b the high-ability worker has dotted indifference curves, and the low-ability worker has the solid indifference curves. The higher isoprofit contour (the concave curve with the short dashed lines that runs through point *H*) corresponds to zero profit for a worker with a higher level of ability. It lies above the profit function for low-ability workers because firms can still earn zero profits on high-ability workers while paying higher wages and offering more flexibility.

A regression through points *M* and *H* would reveal a positively sloped market line, suggesting that high wages and more flexibility go together. A positive regression line implies, at the most naive level, that either wages or choice over hours is viewed by the worker as a "bad" instead of a "good." Of course this would be absurd in the current context. In reality the positive line reflects the fact that firms are willing to offer both higher wages and more choice over hours to higher-ability workers than to low-ability workers. But the underlying indifference curves are negatively sloped for both types of individuals. Both high-ability and low-ability workers are willing to trade flexibility in hours for wages, although perhaps at different rates.

Of course, if the compensation consultant had sufficiently rich data, he could hold ability factors constant. If this were done sufficiently well, the observed market relation would have a negative slope. The researcher would be looking only at points that pertain either to high-ability workers or to low-ability workers but not both. Since all high-ability workers must receive compensation packages that put them on an indifference curve as high as the one through point H, the market line would necessarily have negative slope. The same is true for the market line for low-ability workers. In reality holding ability constant at such a refined level is going to be extremely difficult.

Comparable Worth

The issues just discussed relate directly to the attempts by governments to regulate wage setting in private industry. One example is in the area of comparable worth, where a third party attempts to set wages on the basis of some exogenous index. There is no theoretical basis on which to use index theory as an argument for comparable worth. To the extent that an index is valid, it derives its validity from its basis in market data. However, if the market is already distorted, because of discrimination or other issues, then indexes based on the market will not be sound foundations for any wage-setting policy.

Beyond this point there are a large number of arguments against the use of indexes to set wages.[1] In this context, however, one is particularly relevant. Comparable worth indexes focus on between-job comparisons rather than individual-based or total enterprise comparisons. To the extent that there is ambiguity in the definitions of a "job" (see chapter 7), any job-based index is going to be particularly suspect. For the moment, let us assume that we can agree on the definition of jobs and that this categorization is of relevance to the organization. Focusing on between-job rather than total variation can lead to some absurd interpretations. Consider table 6.1.

There are two jobs in the economy. One is called the male job because it is held by two men and one woman. The other is called the female job

Table 6.1
Comparable worth

	Male job salary		Female job salary
Male 1	$20,000	Female 2	$25,000
Male 2	$20,000	Female 3	$25,000
Female 1	$50,000	Male 3	$10,000
Average	$30,000	Average	$20,000

because it is held by two women and one man. The average salary in the male job is $30,000 a year. The average salary in the female job is only $20,000 a year. Let us suppose that according to some external index, the jobs have equal value. Observing different average salaries in jobs with "equivalent value" would lead us to conclude that there is discrimination against women in this economy. Such a conclusion would be absurd.

First, note that within each job, women are paid more than their male counterparts. In the male job, the men are paid $20,000 and the woman is paid $50,000. In the female job, the women are paid $25,000 and the man is paid $10,000. Thus within each job, women are paid more than men. Second, note that the average wage for women in the economy is $33,333. The average wage for men in the economy is $16,667. Finally, note that there is no man in the economy who makes as much as the lowest-paid woman in the economy.

While this is a stylized example, with extreme numbers, the point is clear. Focusing on between-job variation and ignoring within-job variation gives a totally distorted picture of what is happening within the economy. Even if an index satisfies identification criteria, and even if that index is well measured and unambiguous, this example points out that indexes, at best, focus on between-job rather than within-job, comparisons. Between-job comparisons may be relevant for some considerations, but they are not all encompassing. Other equally or potentially more important considerations come into play in making wage comparisons between individuals.

Beyond the index number issue, wage adjustment via comparable worth is the wrong solution to the problem even if there is a problem. If women earn lower wages because they are in different jobs than men, there are two possible explanations.

First, they may be in those jobs by choice, in which case the lower wages reflect compensating differentials for nonpecuniary attributes. Professors earn less than similarly skilled physicians because being a professor is presumably a nicer (or easier) job. If women earn lower wages than men

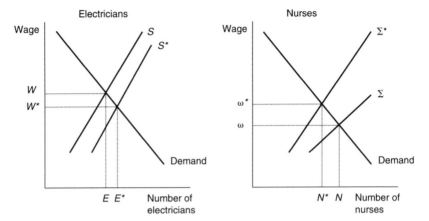

Figure 6.2c

because their jobs are easier, and if men in those jobs also earn low wages because they have opted for an easier job, then no adjustment is warranted. On the contrary, raising the wages of women's jobs would result in a surplus of workers wanting the jobs currently held by women and would cause unemployment.

Second, and alternatively, women may be in low-wage female jobs not because they want to be but because they are excluded from higher-paying male jobs. In this case something is wrong and needs to be remedied. But wage adjustment is the wrong solution. Consider figure 6.2c.

Demand and supply for two occupations, electricians and nurses, are shown. The current supply curves for the two occupations are given by S and Σ for electricians and nurses, respectively. The market wage is W for electricians and ω for nurses. As can be seen, wages of nurses are lower than those of electricians. But this may reflect exclusion of women from electrical work. Suppose that if women were not excluded from electrical work and forced into nursing, the supply of electricians would be S^* and supply of nurses would be Σ^*. The resulting wages would then be W^* and ω^*, which in this case happen to be equal.

What would be the effect of forcing nurses' wages up to those of electricians? If nothing else were done, unemployment of women would result. Since $W > W^*$, setting $\omega = W$ would cause wages of nurses to be above their equilibrium level and supply would exceed demand. The appropriate solution is simply to remove the barrier that prevents women from being electricians. If that barrier were removed, all would be right. There need be no external wage adjustment at all.

Bonuses and Penalties

Should workers be motivated through the use of carrots or sticks? This topic has intrigued psychologists for a long period of time. The best-known work on this subject is by Tversky and Kahneman (1981), who argue that "framing," or the way in which an issue is presented, is central. They claim that the status quo has particular significance for individuals. Bonuses are seen as a positive deviation from the status quo, whereas penalties are seen as a negative deviation from the status quo. Tversky and Kahneman argue, and provide experimental evidence to support the claim, that individuals behave differently when faced with positive reinforcement than when they are faced with negative reinforcement. These issues are of direct relevance to compensation.

Consider two possible compensation schemes. Scheme A pays the worker a monthly salary of $10,000 plus a bonus of $1 for each unit of output produced. Scheme B pays the worker a salary of $15,000 but subtracts $1 for every unit that output falls short of 5,000. (If output exceeds 5,000, the subtracted amount is negative.) The bonus scheme can be written as

$$\text{Bonus:} \quad \text{Pay} = 10{,}000 + q, \tag{6.2}$$

whereas the penalty scheme can be written as

$$\text{Penalty:} \quad \text{Pay} = 15{,}000 - (5{,}000 - q)$$
$$= 10{,}000 + q. \tag{6.3}$$

Obviously these schemes are algebraically equivalent. Further their equivalence is so transparent that it is difficult to believe that the typical worker can be affected by the way in which the compensation formula is presented. Still many, particularly experimental psychologists, argue that the two schemes induce different kinds of behavior. How can this be?

First, let us recognize that the workplace has examples of both penalty and bonus terminology. For example, if a worker arrives at work late he is "docked" pay. Docking a worker's pay fits the language of penalties. The worker receives full pay if he arrives on time but suffers a penalty in the form of a pay reduction for late arrival. Other examples of penalties come from professional sports. A football player who misses practice or gets into an argument with a referee is sometimes fined. A fine is a penalty. But both of these examples could have been restated in terms of bonuses rather than penalties.

The worker who is penalized for arriving late could, as an alternative, be rewarded for arriving on time. Rather than telling the worker that he will lose a half-hour's pay for coming at 8:30 a.m. instead of 8:00 a.m., the worker could be told that he will gain a half-hour in pay if he arrives at 8:00 rather than at 8:30. Of course the take-home pay is exactly the same, irrespective of the choice of wording. Analogously, the football player could be told that if he stays out of trouble and makes all practices, he will receive a bonus above the level of compensation that corresponds to bad behavior pay. Choosing the bonuses and initial pay structure carefully can result in exactly the same payment structure as the fining scheme.

There are many examples of workers being given bonuses. For example, at Christmas time workers are often given bonuses reflecting "appreciation" for good work performed during the year. Salespersons receive bonuses for having reached a particular target. Even these cases could be respecified in terms of penalties, but the language would sound rather offensive. Rather than congratulating someone on good work at Christmas time, the manager would be forced to say, "Good work, Joe. You performed well this year, therefore I am reducing the size of your Christmas penalty." Similarly a satisfied manager would have to tell his salesperson that his fine is being reduced because he had achieved his target. While neither one seems particularly appealing, both convey exactly the same compensation level. Something else must be involved when deciding whether to specify compensation as a bonus or penalty structure.

The framing approach is a somewhat unsatisfying explanation for a number of reasons. First, it is not clear that framing induces different behavior in a compensation environment, when workers think about these numbers over and over again.

Second, even if the choice of language does have different incentive effects, the direction of those differences is not obvious. Some have argued that carrots are better than sticks. Those who believe in risk aversion as an important force might expect sticks to be more powerful. A given dollar deduction hurts a risk-averse worker more than a given dollar increase, if anchored at the same point. The theory of risk aversion really does not speak to this issue because what is at issue is moving along exactly the same section of the utility function. We are simply trying to determine whether starting at the top and moving down to some point induces different behavior from starting at the bottom and moving up to that same point.

Third, it is not clear how the status quo should be defined. For example, if we go back to the bonus and penalty compensation scheme shown in equations (6.2) and (6.3), it is not clear how to define status quo. One might be tempted to define the status quo as $10,000 in (6.2) and $15,000 in (6.3). But there are alternative interpretations of status quo. One notion of status quo would be not $10,000 but the average amount earned by the typical employee. Another definition would have $10,000, even in expression (6.3), because the most simple representation of the penalty scheme does have a constant of $10,000 [see the second line of (6.3)].

Fourth, the theory is not a good theory unless it can predict practice in the real world. Satisfactory theory must predict when a firm will use bonus terminology and when a firm will use penalty terminology. Unless it does, it is an incomplete theory at best.

An obvious thought is that the language of bonuses and penalties is chosen to reflect expectations. A penalty is a negative deviation from some expected level and a bonus is a positive deviation from some expected level. The argument goes that firms would like to induce workers to behave at some expected level, and everything above it is gravy. Formally this means that the cost of erring on the downside is higher than the benefit of erring on the upside. While this may very well be true, the question remains as to why language, rather than direct pecuniary compensation, is used to convey the message. It would be quite easy for a firm to pay a higher amount to workers who arrive on time than to those who arrive late. If it is important to be at the firm when the shift starts, then a nonlinear wage structure will induce the desired behavior. The first hour's wage rate would be higher than the subsequent hour's wage rates, and the difference in the wages would reflect the true value to the firm of being on time. This would give workers the appropriate signals, and they could choose to arrive or not to arrive optimally, depending on the alternative uses of their time.[2]

An alternative theory is that bonuses and penalties refer to different kinds of nonlinear compensation schemes. Bonuses are used when output below some level has no adverse consequences, and penalties are used when output above some particular level has no beneficial consequences. To see the point, consider the following two examples. First, workers are docked pay when they arrive late to work. But they are not paid extra for arriving early. Thus the compensation scheme is the one shown in figure 6.3. Arrival times are shown on the horizontal axis with the latest arrival time shown at the origin. If the worker arrives at 5:00 p.m., he receives zero. If he arrives at 8:00 a.m., he receives the full day's pay and the scheme is linear between 5:00 p.m. and 8:00 a.m. However, when the worker arrives at 7:30 a.m., no additional pay, beyond that received by a

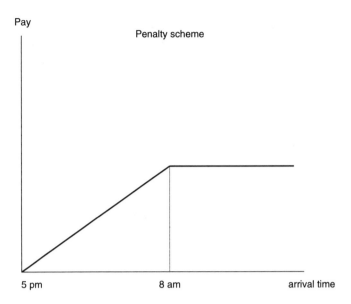

Figure 6.3

worker who arrives at 8:00, is earned. The reason of course is that firms place no value on having workers arrive before their shift starts, and so they do not compensate workers for early arrival. Thus output, or input as measured by arrival time, has no additional value beyond that of arriving at 8:00 a.m. The nonlinear compensation scheme causes arrival times to bunch around 8:00 a.m. No one arrives before 8:00 a.m. (except by mistake); a few do choose to arrive late. But the kink in the compensation scheme induces most arrival at 8:00 a.m.

Consider the bonus scheme, as shown in figure 6.4. Its usefulness is illustrated by the following story: Suppose that an absent-minded individual leaves his automobile's headlights on and returns to find a dead battery. In order to get the car started, it must be pushed. If the car moves less than five miles an hour, the probability that it will start is zero. However, for every mile per hour that the car is pushed above five, the probability that it starts is an increasing and linear function of speed. One possible compensation scheme is to pay the worker twenty dollars and then a bonus of one dollar per mile per hour above five miles per hour. This fits the language of bonus because the twenty-dollar amount is fixed and the worker does not receive any "extra" compensation until he hits his target level of five miles per hour.

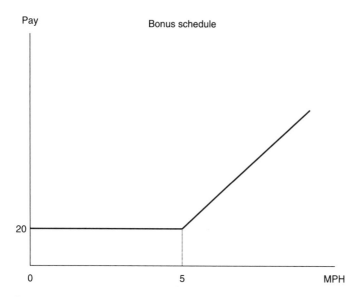

Figure 6.4

This scheme is chosen because all levels of output between zero and five are equivalent as far as the car's owner is concerned. Pushing the car at four miles per hour does no more for the automobile owner than pushing it at one mile per hour. In this case output or input below some crucial level imposes no additional costs on the owner.

The interpretation of bonuses and penalties as nonlinear compensation schemes with essentially reverse patterns of pay may or may not be correct. But this interpretation has the advantage that it is a testable theory. For example, the theory implies that penalty structures should be used when additional input beyond some target level has no value. It fits the case of docking pay quite well. It also suggests that bonuses should be used when input or output levels below some crucial amount have no value. This fits the automobile example but may be less appropriate to the case of Christmas bonuses. Still the virtues that the theory is testable and yields explicit predictions are important ones.

Macroeconomic Issues

Personnel economics, and theories of internal labor markets in general, have implications for macroeconomic behavior as well. Macroeconomic issues are not the topic of this book, but two issues are addressed. Both the topics of efficiency wages and insider/outsider labor market behavior are closely tied to the personnel questions discussed so far. Let us consider each in turn.

Efficiency Wages

Efficiency wage theory has attracted a large following over the past few years, primarily for two reasons. First, the onslaught of rational expectations weakened the appeal of Keynesian economics. Efficiency wage theory was viewed as a way to resurrect a troubled theory and restore the foundations for involuntary unemployment. Efficiency wage theory generates involuntary unemployment in the same way that rigid wages did in the past. The advantage of efficiency wage theory over other forms of rigid wages is that the story is appealing, which is the second reason for the interest in efficiency wage theory. Introspection suggests that we often pay babysitters and others high wages, perhaps more than necessary, in order to induce them to behave in a more productive manner. But the story of incentives is often confounded with the story of involuntary unemployment. In order for efficiency wage theory to hold, there are three necessary ingredients.

First, higher wages must cause higher productivity. For example, efficiency wages are high wages paid to workers to induce them to put forth more effort. This requirement amounts to nothing more than positively sloped labor supply. By itself it has little or nothing to do with involuntary unemployment. Higher wages induce higher hours of work, and higher wages per hour are likely to induce higher effort per hour as well. Standard labor supply theory gives this implication. It is neither the creation nor property of efficiency wage theory.

Second, there must be a queue for the job. That is, wages must be set above the market level, so that workers are induced to queue up for particular slots. While this is a necessary ingredient for efficiency wage theory to hold, it is not sufficient. Any employer who makes a mistake and pays more than the market wage will be flooded with applicants, whether that high wage was part of a conscious efficiency wage strategy or not.

Thus, we add the third requirement: The high-efficiency-wage policy must result in more profit than does a low-wage policy. Herein lies the empirical problem. The way by which the existence of efficiency wages is documented usually is to show that a change brought about the results implied by efficiency wage theory.[3] But if an employer changed his wage policy, then the policy was wrong before the change, after the change, or in both situations. To determine that efficiency wage motivations lie behind the theory, it is necessary to document that the high-wage, high-output strategy was more profitable than the low-wage, low-output strategy.

In fact the situation is even tougher. Efficiency wage theory really does not predict unemployment but rather that individuals will move into a secondary sector.[4] Workers who are in jobs in the secondary sector earn low wages, put forth low levels of effort, and are generally less happy than those who work in the primary sector. But firms must be indifferent between employing workers from the secondary labor market and from the primary labor market. In equilibrium, zero profit implies that firms will move from one sector to another until product prices change enough to restore equilibrium. This means that the profitability of low-wage firms is no lower than the profitability of high-wage firms. Some other instruments are needed in order to predict whether a firm will choose the low-wage or high-wage policy. Only when those instruments are identified can efficiency wage theory truly be tested. This is a tall order. It will be difficult to distinguish between efficiency wage theory and an alternative view that simply says that there are high-ability and low-ability workers who sort across firms. There need be no involuntary unemployment.

Indeed the intrigue with efficiency wage theory, which in large part is based on the attraction to incentive theory, is misplaced. The payment of incentive wages does not imply that markets do not clear. Most of this book has discussed incentive mechanisms, all of which are market clearing. For example, in the tournament framework wage levels are set such that workers are indifferent between working at the tournament job and working at some alternative or taking leisure. When workers are paid along an upward-sloping age-earnings profile to elicit effort, wages are sufficiently low initially to make workers just indifferent between working at this job and working elsewhere. Again, no queuing is necessary. In fact the upward-sloping experience-earnings profile discussed earlier has the appearance of an efficiency wage in many ways. Older workers are paid more than their marginal product, and more than they can obtain at some alternative job. If they lose their current job, they will suffer a large wage loss as they move either into the secondary sector or take leisure, all of which seems consistent with efficiency wages. The major difference of course is that the market clears when workers are paid along an upward-sloping age-earnings profile. At the outset worker wages are sufficiently low to clear markets.

Finally, when workers are paid piece rates, more effort results in more compensation, but a linear wage structure is sufficient to make workers just indifferent between the piece rate job and their alternatives. In fact it is exactly the use of a piece rate structure that motivates most of the incorrect discussion on efficiency wages.

Suppose that the piece rate discussed in chapter 2 were equal to

$$Pay = \beta q \qquad\qquad\qquad (6.4)$$

instead of, as in (2.1),

$$Pay = \alpha + \gamma q.$$

The parameter β in (6.4) must serve two functions. First, it must affect the marginal incentives of workers. Second, it must determine the total amount of compensation that the worker receives. In general, it is impossible to set β in a way that satisfies two constraints. If β is chosen so as to bring about efficiency on the effort margin, it will generally be too high to clear the market. But of course this is a direct result of failing to use a slightly modified compensation scheme. If the intercept α in (2.1) is allowed to be nonzero, then, in general, it is possible to find a compensation scheme that provides incentives and clears the market.

A number of researchers have tied having a negative α to the issue of bonding. In chapter 2, α had a negative value, but fees from workers were never collected. In fact, most of the time, bonds are merely a distraction. In equilibrium $\alpha + \beta q$ will surely be positive, so there is no requirement that a worker put up a bond initially. Furthermore a shirking strategy where q falls below its optimal level is not, in general, optimal for the worker even if the firm cannot extract payment from the worker to the firm. To see this, note that when α is negative, no choice of effort less than the optimal one provides the worker with greater utility than the optimal effort, even if the worker receives zero for implied negative compensation. Zero compensation, which is paid when workers would have received negative compensation, will always be viewed by the workers as inferior to market compensation for the optimal level of effort. So the issue of bonding is, at least in this piece rate context, beside the point.[5]

Reputation and Ex post Settling Up

It is sometimes unnecessary to provide internal motivators to induce workers to put forth sufficient effort. If worker reputation can be established, then a worker has an incentive to put forth effort, not because of what he gets from this job this period but because this period's effort affects next period's wage. For example, in the banking industry, where a banker's performance can be observed readily by those who are using his services, the banker has an incentive to perform well. Good performance can result in a subsequent job offer from the firms with which he has had contact. His wage increases, either because the bank raises his compensation to compete with outside offers or because he leaves to accept the new higher paying job. Thus he is paid ex post for performance that was rendered earlier.

The issue of ex post settling up was first explored by Fama (1980) and reexamined by Holmstrom (1982a). Fama and Holmstrom both conclude that under certain circumstances, which relate to statistical properties of the production process, the market will perfectly reward a worker for his performance, whether or not it is done internally. Fama is somewhat more sanguine about the universality of this proposition than is Holmstrom, who criticizes the proposition on the basis of its required conditions. At an empirical level Gibbons and Murphy (1990) show that the compensation that a CEO receives in subsequent periods and his probability of retaining his job depend on earlier (relative) performance.

Insider-Outsider Theories

Insider-outsider theory is to my mind somewhat more attractive than efficiency wage theory.[6] It relies on the difference between ex post trades and ex ante trades, which arise when workers have spent some time at a particular firm. It is built on more solid micro-foundations than efficiency wage theory but also requires some assumptions.

Firm-specific human capital creates a wedge between the value of insiders and the value of outsiders, as do hiring costs or any other factors that distinguish between new and old workers. Whether involuntary unemployment is a result depends on the assumptions made about the transfer of property rights. To the extent that insiders restrict employment inefficiently, there are gains to be had by selling some jobs to outsiders and pocketing the rents. Unfortunately, it may not be possible for workers to sell their rights to new jobs and still maintain their power. To the extent that auctioning off jobs undermines the ability of insiders to affect the decisions of the firm, an inefficiently low level of employment can result. This is akin to the results on worker-owned firms, where workers who share in the value of the firm go for average rather than marginal product. Of course this inefficiency can be eliminated, but doing so may also eliminate the ability of workers to extract rents.

Worker Turnover

Any choice of compensation scheme has implications for worker turnover. The first coherent theory of turnover was presented by Becker (1962), who argued that investment in firm-specific human capital would reduce turnover. Compensation was such that firms and workers split the costs and benefits of the investment. Because each party derived some returns, workers and firms would have an incentive to remain together.

In most labor markets, quits and layoffs are not infrequent events. Workers leave the firm to accept positions at other organizations that offer higher wages. But the worker's current organization need not and generally will not remain passive while other firms attempt to pirate its workers. It is important to understand the strategy that firms use and the resulting turnover patterns. The following game-theoretic model illustrates the kinds of forces operating in a work environment where turnover is a possibility.[7]

Much worker turnover occurs without an intervening spell of unemployment. Search theory is designed to analyze employment of workers who are being drawn from a pool of unemployed workers. The difference between being employed and unemployed is that an employed worker can go to his current employer and announce that he has an outside wage offer. An employer has the option of responding to this offer, and the response affects the likelihood that the worker will move to a new firm. Outsiders, knowing this, will tailor their own offers accordingly. Specifically they will take into account that there is information in the decision by the current firm to match or not match the outside offer. But the analysis of whether and under which circumstances the firm will respond is not part of standard search theory. Thus a different analysis must be used to examine the most common form of turnover among workers who quit their jobs, namely turnover that occurs without a spell of unemployment.

Important in determining a firm's strategy is information. Its information, and what it can infer from the moves of others, affect both its desire to raid another firm's worker and its willingness to counter a raid by matching outside offers. The modeling of this information provides insight into labor turnover and into firms' best offer-matching strategies.

Let there be two firms j and k, with j being the worker's current employer. In April j declares the wage W that it will offer the worker for the year beginning September 1. In May k may decide to raid j for this worker, offering a wage higher than W. Between May and September j and k can make counteroffers, and the worker ends up going to the firm that makes the highest offer. Trivial mobility costs mean that j wins all ties.

The worker is worth M_j and M_k at firms j and k, respectively:

$$M_j = M + S,$$

$$M_k = M,$$

where M is the worker's general skill and S is skill specific to firm j. A negative value of S implies that the worker is better suited to firm k. Both M and S are random variables. To make things simple, consider the case where M is distributed uniformly on the interval $[0, 1]$ and S is distributed uniformly on the interval $[-\alpha/2, \alpha/2]$. As α goes to zero, the firm-specific component becomes unimportant. As will be seen, when $\alpha = 0$, no turn-over occurs.

Information is what makes turnover occur. With some probability P_j, firm j knows M_j; otherwise, j knows only the distribution of M_j. Similarly, with some probability P_k, firm k knows M_k; otherwise, k knows only the distribution of M_k. Generally one would expect that $P_j > P_k$, that the firm knows its own worker's productivity better than other firms know its worker's productivity. But this assumption is not essential. We state without proof or derivation the main principles and results of the theory.[8]

1. Some workers will be raided and lost. They tend to be the high-ability workers who are underpaid by their current firm. The firm calls out a wage W. But some workers have $M > W$, and some have $M < W$. Outsiders will not go after a worker unless $M > W$. This means that the workers who are left at the end of the May-through-August auction process tend to be from the bottom of the distribution. Knowing this, firms adjust W appropriately in April. In this example, firms would not offer $W = \frac{1}{2}$. While $\frac{1}{2}$ is the mean of the unconditional distribution of $M + S$, it is not the mean productivity of workers who are left at j at the end of the process. Better workers are raided, so j must adjust its wage offer down-ward to take this into account.

2. Firm k actually hopes that j knows the productivity of a worker that k is raiding. If j is ignorant of a worker's productivity, then j's best strategy is to match the offer of k. Since k would not raid unless it had information that the worker was underpaid, the raid signals to j's management that the worker must be worth more than j thought. It is always best for j to mimic k's offers when j is uninformed. Thus ignorant firms match offers on their workers.

However, j may be informed of a particular worker's productivity. It will match k's offers up to the actual value of M_j. But in cases where $S < 0$, k will be willing to offer more to the worker than j because the worker is better suited to firm k than to firm j. This implies the following:

a. Raids are successful only when a worker is better suited to the raiding firm. Thus raids are efficient.

b. The raiding and counteroffer process is a necessary part of worker sorting. Without it, firms would not engage in voluntary exchange that would result in efficient sorting. Instead, they would attempt to pawn off lemons.[9]

c. The best policy for an ignorant firm is to match the "genuine" offers of outsiders. Genuine offers may be difficult to determine, however. The worker has an incentive to pay an outsider to make a bogus offer, which the worker would use only to raise his salary at firm j.

3. Workers who remain in the job (or at the firm) and are not raided tend to be drawn from the bottom part of the distribution. Thus within-job wages should decline with tenure. Empirical evidence bears this out and will be discussed in the next chapter.

4. Wage dispersion is high in occupations where turnover is high. High turnover reflects high levels of P_j and P_k, namely that firms are well informed about their workers' productivity levels. (Recall that ignorant firms match offers, so no turnover occurs.) When many workers leave the firm, those who are left are from the bottom of the distribution. They receive low salaries, and those who are raided receive high ones. Thus more information implies more turnover, more inequality, and also higher efficiency as workers are sorted to their best uses.

5. In some early work I found that workers who searched for jobs while unemployed actually received lower wages when they obtained a job than those who did not search during their period of unemployment. The model predicts this result. If two workers are out of work for three months and neither finds a job, the information implications are more negative for the worker who was searching. Less can be inferred about a worker's low-ability level when the worker was not looking.

This also implies that being laid off during a recession reduces subsequent wages by less than being laid off during an expansion. Since many workers are laid off during recessions, less can be inferred about a worker's low productivity from the layoff.[10] Some recent work by Gibbons and Katz (1991) finds support for this proposition.

7   The Job

The neoclassical theory of production gives no explicit role to jobs. Firms hire labor, combine it with capital, and produce output according to some production function. Labor is treated as a continuous variable. Furthermore the description of specific tasks assigned to a given worker is no less vague. This traditional view contrasts sharply with the way that managers view the firm. Human resources managers think in terms of slots or jobs, and think of these slots or jobs as being fundamental to the organization of the firm.

While jobs have no role in traditional production theory, they have become important, even if implicitly, in the economics of personnel. In this section the various definitions of jobs are explored, and the significance and implications of these views of the job for labor market behavior are discussed. Also presented is some recent empirical evidence, which bears on the relevance of the various job definitions.[1]

A basic question is, Does the person define the job or does the job define the person?[2] The difference in viewpoint distinguishes human capital views of labor markets from institutional views of labor markets. According to institutionalists, jobs are defined first. In the most extreme form all workers are perfect substitutes. The allocation of individuals to jobs is arbitrary and generally reflects luck or other non-job-related factors.[3]

The human capital view, dominant since the 1960s, focuses primarily on the supply side. Workers invest in human capital, which augments their productivity and makes them more attractive to firms. Their wages increase as a result. But workers carry their skills to the workplace, and there is little attention paid to the fit between workers and the particular workplace. Human capital is measured in efficiency units so that workers are viewed to be perfect substitutes.

For example, suppose that the following relation holds:

$$\ln W = \alpha + \beta A + \gamma E$$

$$= 1.3 + 0.08S + 0.06E,$$

(7.1)

where W is the hourly wage rate, S is the number of years of schooling completed, and E is the number of years of work experience. This earnings regression, which has become standard (see Mincer 1974), says that increasing schooling completion by one year will raise wages by about 8 percent. Schooling and experience are like factors in the production of human capital. Because of the linear specification they are perfect substitutes, with one year of schooling being worth 33 percent more than one year of experience. Note that this regression does not have included in it anything that relates to the job itself. The characteristics of the job, or measures of worker fit, are left out, at least in this most basic formulation.

More sophisticated views of human capital have been produced that move somewhere in between the traditional human capital and traditional institutional analyses. For example, Jovanovic (1979) discusses matching workers to firms on the basis of firm-specific components. Sicherman (1987) treats human capital as being occupation specific and thereby attaches some significance to the slotting of workers into their given occupations. But the essence of human capital theory is that the job is unimportant. Wages and wealth are determined by the individuals' skills. Occupation and industry variables are secondary and almost an embarrassment to the theory. The fact that occupation and industry often enter significantly into wage equations is something that human capital theory rarely explains.

The slot or integer problem associated with jobs is generally ignored by production theory. Furthermore, when considering differences in labor quality, the focus is generally on the skills of the worker rather than on the job to which the worker is assigned. Thus human capital and standard production theory minimize any emphasis on jobs or slots.

This view is quite different from the one held by the typical businessperson. Deans, department heads, and personnel managers alike are generally aware of their slot allocations. While there may some flexibility in tailoring jobs to individuals within the firm, the fact remains that managers often speak in terms of hiring workers into given jobs.

The notion of jobs as being important in the organization is not alien to personnel economics. There are a number of theoretical insights, some of which have already been discussed, that draw upon the job as an important concept. Some of those are discussed in the following section.

Tournaments

The tournament model, as already presented, defines a job as a wage slot. In chapter 3 an example of two workers competing for a boss's job and an operator's job was presented. In that model there were two slots irrespective of the outcome of the contest. No matter how well or poorly each of the workers performed, one worker would be assigned to the boss's job, while the other worker would be assigned to the operator's job.

Neither "boss" nor "operator" connoted any particular task assignment. In fact, strictly speaking, the tournament model, as presented, had only one period and both individuals were performing exactly the same task during that period. This point is important because it makes clear how jobs are endogenous within a firm. It is quite easy, for example, to change the wage distribution within a firm simply by changing the number of jobs at each level. In fact that practice is followed in many organizations. When a secretary is no longer receiving a high enough wage to keep him, a new job is sometimes opened up called administrative assistant. By allowing secretaries to compete for this additional administrative assistant slot, the average wage has increased, and the shape of the firm's hierarchical pyramid has been changed. As long as it is unnecessary to change the task associated with a particular job, firms have virtually unlimited flexibility over the wage structure within the organization. If jobs and tasks need not go together, it is always possible for a firm to provide motivation to workers simply by creating more potential slots for promotion.

This point has already been mentioned in an earlier context. When discussing upward-sloping experience-earnings profiles, it was argued that a potential motivation problem results when workers attain a level at which they're virtually certain to remain for the rest of their careers. One way out of the dilemma is to have within-job wage growth that is associated with performance, thus the upward-sloping age-earnings profile is used. An alternative is simply to create additional promotion slots that lie between the next highest level and the current level of the job. Workers who perform well then can be promoted to those higher slots.

The difference between using promotion and using an upward-sloping experience-earnings profile is that promotions are based on relative performance, whereas raises within the job are generally based on an individual's absolute performance. All workers can receive a merit increase, or no workers can. There are no slots necessarily associated with this kind of motivation scheme. Thus the distinction between promotion and upward-sloping age-earnings profile does have real content. It is not merely a question of job definition.[4]

In the promotion context the most important aspect is that the number of slots is fixed in advance. Wages are assigned to the slot, not the individual. This scheme is quite different from a piece rate arrangement, where a worker's job assignment is independent of the job assignments of his peers. Another difference is that in a piece rate scheme, compensation moves continually with output. In a tournament scheme, compensation is fixed in advance and attached to the slots, not to the performance of the individuals who occupy them. Tournaments create a somewhat discontinuous distribution of earnings that is observable.

Carmichael (1981) argues that the association of wages to slots makes employers better able to commit to their promises to pay higher wages if a particular standard is met. When slots are established in advance, the employer must assign one individual to the high-wage slot and another individual to the low-wage slot. Under these circumstances employers gain little by lying about the performance of workers. In fact the reverse is true. If employers simply assigned workers to slots randomly, then the tournament compensation structure would have no effect on incentives. Recall that for workers to be motivated to put forth effort, it is necessary that increasing effort affects the probability of winning the contest. The first-order condition in the typical tournament is reproduced here:

$$(W_1 - W_2)\frac{\partial P}{\partial \mu} = C'(\mu).$$

The left-hand side is the spread times the change in the probability of winning associated with an increment of effort. The right-hand side is simply the marginal cost of effort. If supervisors are arbitrary in choosing workers for promotion, then the $\partial P/\partial \mu$ becomes 0 and effort is zero for any given wage spread.

It is a fixed-slot structure that distinguishes tournaments from other kinds of compensation schemes based on relative performance. As was pointed out in chapter 3, another reason for using the tournament is to difference out common noise that affects all workers in the work force in a similar way. Since risk-averse workers do not like their compensation to vary with conditions over which they have no control, tournaments may provide a compensation method that is more attractive to risk-averse workers. But tournaments are not the only way to difference out the common noise. An alternative is to pay a piece rate that indexes compensation to, say, the mean of the work force. Doing so would difference out common noise, but it would not have the commitment advantage discussed by Carmichael.

A payment scheme that is based on output relative to some mean does not conform to our notion of jobs or slots. While this kind of relative compensation scheme differences out common noise, it does so without setting up explicit jobs or wage categories. In the tournament model, wages and slots are designated in advance before output is known. In tournaments, one and only one individual gets the top prize or top job. One and only one gets the second prize, the second-best job, and so forth. In other relative compensation schemes that are continuous, the structure of wages and positions evolved ex post rather than ex ante. Thus tournament theory involves jobs per se, whereas other relative compensation schemes do not.

In the tournament framework the number of jobs in the firm, and their hierarchical structure, satisfy only one goal: the provision of incentives for the work force. If workers were risk neutral and of identical ex ante ability, then two jobs would be sufficient irrespective of the number of workers in a firm. First-best effort could be induced, either by classifying all but the best worker as operators and the best worker as boss, or by classifying all but the worst worker as bosses and the worst worker as operator. Of course the corresponding wage structures would differ in the two scenarios, but there need be no more than two jobs to generate perfect incentives.

In the real world there are many more than two jobs in the typical firm. There are a number of ways to reconcile this, even in the context of tournament theory. First, if workers are risk averse, then the existence of only two jobs creates a very risky payoff function. Workers either win big or lose big depending on the luck of the draw. Green and Stokey (1983) have shown that a nonlinear piece rate is always preferred to tournaments on risk considerations alone when common noise is not an issue. To the extent that a multistage tournament differences out common noise, and also approximates a nonlinear piece rate, it will be preferred over a tournament with only two jobs.

Heterogeneity is also a factor. If the process evolves somewhat slowly and workers have different abilities, then the two-job incentive structure induces all workers to give up. Consider the following example, again drawing from tennis. Suppose that sixteen players begin a tournament.

One of the players is Andre Agassi. Another player is a relatively un-known rising star from Minnesota named Sven Svensson. Svensson has played Agassi on a number of occasions and has never come close to beating him. Still he feels that he has a shot at beating almost everyone in the tournament, with the exception of Agassi.

If there are only two prizes in that the winner receives one prize and everyone else receives another, Svensson will give up. Since he has no chance of beating Agassi, he will reduce his effort and simply accept a lower spot in the tournament. He could accept the losers' prize and save his energy for another day. Knowing this, Agassi will put forth less energy in his matches. This behavior is not optimal when the marginal cost of effort is less than the value of output; it can be avoided by stocking a tournament with some intermediate prizes. If, for example, places one through five are given additional prize money, with all the rest of the field receiving a consolation prize, then Svensson will have every incentive to try for one of the higher-placed prizes, even if he all but rules out de-feating Agassi. Heterogeneity among workers creates a reason for having several hierarchical levels within the firm. To prevent workers from giving up, it is necessary to make sure that they have some chance at a prize or wage rate higher than the one that they are currently receiving.

When individuals have different ability levels, a handicapping system can offset the adverse incentives associated with mixing types. For risk-neutral workers the result is that the less able worker is given credit that eliminates half of the difference between himself and his superior rival. The better player is still more likely to win, but the fact that chances are improved for the poorer player induces both to put forth the efficient level of effort. Alternatively, players can be allowed to compete fairly, but prizes can be different. A system of reverse discrimination, where a win by the less able player results in a bigger prize (higher wage) than a win by the more able player, can also provide appropriate incentives. Both solu-tions work, but implementation requires that ability be observable, which may be a major impediment to their widespread use.

Once ability is allowed to vary across individuals, there is another simple way to justify a hierarchical job structure. To the extent that it is important for the high-ability person to be placed at the top of the firm, running individuals through a tournament may provide information on workers' relative ability. In his Ph.D. dissertation Gibbs (1989) models a structure that both provides incentives and sorts workers according to their ability. At each round of the contest the pool of contestants contains individuals of higher and higher ability, so the top is dominated by the most able workers. Gibbs's work builds on the incentive structure in Rosen (1986) and attempts to deal with the sorting and incentive problems simultaneously.[5]

Hierarchies

In addition to tournament theory, which gives an incentive motivation for a hierarchical wage structure, there is another literature that attempts to explain the firm's hierarchical structure. There are two thrusts to this literature. One thinks of supervisory positions as exerting a direct effect on their subordinates. A high-quality supervisor affects the output of all his subordinates, perhaps because he is able to give crucial advice or training to those working under him. The literature on span of control[6] takes as given the number of subordinates per supervisor. But the size of the firm, the number of levels in it, and the quality of the work force are all endogenous.

An alternative theory of hierarchy builds on statistical analyses. An example of this approach is Sah and Stiglitz (1986). They model the firm as an organization that screens projects. The goal is to trade off type I and type II error: The firm wants neither to reject good projects or accept bad ones. By structuring the firm vertically versus horizontally, a different mix of errors is obtained.

In this hierarchical framework the role of the supervisors is to screen projects that are passed up by their subordinates. This model fits well within a common structure in sales organizations where salespersons must report to a sales manager to get a final sale approved. The salesperson does most of the footwork, bringing in the customer and setting up the deal. After the deal has been negotiated, the salesperson goes to the sales manager for final approval. In many contexts this is merely a bargaining strategy that allows the salesperson to make the sales manager the "bad guy." But in other contexts it serves the genuine function of supervision, giving the supervisor the right to reject badly negotiated deals.

In fact one can attempt to explain the rules and structure of department stores along these lines. When one goes to a large department store, individual salespeople do not have the authority to renegotiate price, presumably because owners believe that low-level workers are not capable of doing so with the firm's interest at heart. In smaller organizations the salesperson is often in a position to negotiate price because he reports more directly to the higher-level manager. Thus with the delegation of authority often go the much more detailed and prescribed rules about behavior. Since delegation implies less control, formal rules must substitute for direct supervision.

Theories of hierarchy provide a rationale for jobs that is based on a production perhaps completely independent of incentives. In span of control theories, and statistical theories of project choice, there is no reference to effort. Usually effort is given exogenously and determined strictly by the ability of the underlying work force. But jobs play a crucial role in hierarchical theories because jobs constraints limit the ability of a particular worker to exercise control over his environment.

Insurance

Economic theories that focus on insurance and work sharing have implicit in them some notion of jobs. Inherent in insurance models is the trade-off between hours and heads. If work sharing were done, say, by reducing everyone's hours rather than laying off selected workers, then another kind of insurance would be achieved. But the macroeconomic literature that focuses on layoffs and insurance assumes that, for the most part, there is an inability to trade hours reduction for layoff of individuals.[7] Behind this is the idea that cutting employment, rather than reducing number of hours, is efficient, presumably because there is a fixed cost either in production of goods or in the consumption of leisure that makes it desirable to have jobs of fixed length. If the fixed cost of going to work is sufficiently high, or if the fixed cost of setting up the workplace for a given individual is sufficiently high, then it will not pay to have shortened hours for all individuals. Instead, it would be better to have "jobs" of a specified time period and to fit workers into these particular slots.

The assumptions necessary to justify an inability to trade hours for heads are not unreasonable. Few individuals go on one-day vacations to exotic resorts, and firms are unwilling to allow a worker to work for fifteen minutes at a time, simply because the setup costs are too high.

The insurance literature gives little focus to the identity of individuals who hold the job. In these theories jobs are important and workers are regarded as interchangeable, much along the lines of earlier institutional analyses. Little attention is paid to the level of skill or other characteristics that determine the order of layoff. Usually some seniority system is assumed, or the individual who was laid off is assumed to be selected randomly from some distribution. But the key consideration here is that jobs vary over the business cycle and that the concept of the slot, rather than the total number of hours worked, is important.

Hedonics

It is possible to define jobs in terms of their nonpecuniary characteristics. A job may describe a collection of attributes that are associated with the work environment. This approach is closest to that on which index theory is based. For the purposes of constructing an index, a job is defined as an environment in which all the relative nonpecuniary characteristics are the same. Compensation consulting firms emphasize the relation of jobs to their nonpecuniary characteristics. There is assumed to be perfect substitutability of nonpecuniary characteristics within a job but imperfect substitutions across jobs. Compensation consultants adjust for supply side factors as well as for demand factors. Supply factors are often measured by variables that relate to pleasantness of work.

For the most part demand side characteristics are the ones that define the job. For example, some jobs have more variable employment than others. In large part this is based on the industry in which the job is located. But the pattern of variability in the job is usually thought to derive from demand conditions rather than from supply conditions. Frequent layoffs are common in manufacturing, not because individuals who work in manufacturing prefer frequent layoffs but because the demand for manufactured goods is cyclically sensitive.

Also jobs with significant safety hazards pay higher wages as an equalizing difference.[8] Again the compensating differential is associated with the job itself, not with the individuals who hold it. Risky jobs pay high wages because the jobs themselves have inherent safety problems associated with them not because the workers who hold those jobs are clumsy and clumsiness is a desirable trait.

Investment

Human capital theory focuses on the supply side, but even human capital theory offers a role for the notion of a job. One possible definition of a job is that it is a particular investment opportunity. Some jobs offer greater opportunities for advancement than others, in large part because they are associated with more training than other jobs. In some occupations the acquisition of human capital on the job is extremely important. In other occupations it is much less important. One possibility is to define jobs by the opportunities for investment available to workers. The choice of a job is essentially a choice over an investment profile.[9]

But there is a distinction between this view of jobs and the view that most institutional analyses and other theories take. Unlike other theories that deal with job structure, human capital analysis does not assume that the number of slots is determined ex ante. Slots can be adjusted to suit the number of investors who show up in a given period. Thus the firm has complete flexibility over the number of slots, at least to the extent that it reaches decreasing returns to scale.

The Job as a Set of Tasks

The production approach is to define jobs as a collection of tasks. When tasks are assigned to particular jobs and individuals then are allocated to fill them, the firm's technology is partitioned in a particular way. In some ways this is the most traditional way to think about jobs and perhaps the way that corresponds most closely to what personnel managers have in mind. There are things that need to be done at the firm and individuals are hired to perform those particular tasks.

A question remains, however, as to whether the tasks associated with a particular job are determined in advance or whether they are dependent on the individual who fills the job. My sense is that in most organizations it is some convex combination of the two. An individual may be hired to fill a particular job with which is associated a set of tasks. Once the individual is in the job, the job is tailored to fit the characteristics of the individual. If the incumbent turns out to be extremely able, the definition of the job expands and tasks that were in a domain of other jobs become included in this one. A worker who is somewhat less able may have his job redefined, particularly in the first few months on the job, and salary may be adjusted as well over the long haul.

While there is not a great deal of literature that relates to the association of tasks with jobs, there are a few papers on this topic. The early work has focused on comparative versus absolute advantage,[10] with the more modern work focusing on complementarity.[11] These theories attempt to examine how tasks may be grouped within the firm into particular jobs and then further to decide which individuals or which types of individuals will be assigned to those jobs.

One of the few papers to deal with task assignments is by Holmstrom and Milgrom (1991), who argue that tasks should be grouped on the basis of their observability. They make the clever point that if one task is observable but another is not, then a worker who is paid on the basis of the observable task will substitute toward it and away from the unobservable one. If observable tasks are grouped with other observable tasks, and unobservable ones with unobservable ones, some of the incentive difficulties can be avoided.

Although the point is a valid one, it is doubtful that it goes very far to explain the grouping of tasks in jobs. Technology is likely to be much more important than the incentive issue. For example, professors teach and do research on the same subject not because the output of each is observable but because the production of research and teaching are complementary. Similarly the farm worker who selects the fruit to be picked also does the actual picking. It is conceivable that there are separate spotters, who determine which fruit is to be picked, and pickers, who do the actual picking. But the tasks are grouped into the one job because separate spotting and picking would necessitate duplication of effort. Spotting is difficult to monitor because one cannot easily estimate the number of good fruits that the spotter missed. The output of picking is easily observable. The Holmstrom-Milgrom point suggests therefore that spotting and picking should not be paired, but technological considerations probably dominate in dictating job structure.

Implications for Analysis

The advantage of thinking in terms of jobs, rather than standard supply side characteristics, is that the institutional aspects lead the researcher to ask very different questions. Some of these questions and some preliminary findings are detailed below.

Job Assignment and Lifetime Wealth

If jobs are important, then assignment to a particular job affects a given individual's wealth. If jobs matter, then knowledge of all the relevant individual characteristics is not sufficient to explain individual earnings. Suppose that the worker lands a position by accident. One view holds that the mere fact that the individual has experience in that position should be a factor in explaining lifetime earnings. The alternative view says that the job path is irrelevant in that once underlying characteristics such as educational background, work experience, and possibly ability are known, wages are determined.

The evidence against the most extreme human capital view is strong. As mentioned earlier, Sicherman's dissertation, which is an attempt to recast human capital in a somewhat more "occupational" light, establishes the importance of occupations in the determination of earnings. In a slightly different vein Groshen (1991) and Blau (1984) found that virtually all of the female-male wage differential can be attributed to job assignment, rather than to within-job differences between genders.

Using data from an individual firm, I found that a particular American firm, which has approximately 20,000 employees, is most usefully categorized as having 134 jobs.[12] An analysis of variance using jobs, defined as being one of these 134 numerical titles, explains over 80 percent of the variation in wages within the firm. Thus, once job title (down to the level of 134 jobs) is known, only 20 percent of residual wage variation remains. This does not say that human capital variables are unimportant. It may be that human capital variables are the key determinants of job assignment. However, most earnings regressions that use education and experience as independent variables can explain only about 25 percent of the total variation in earnings. It is unlikely therefore that human capital variables can explain very much about job assignment in this particular data set.

Baker, Gibbs, and Holmstrom (1993, 1994a,b) have performed similar analyses on jobs from another large firm. Their results suggest the importance of individual ability variation and human capital accumulation. In particular, they find that those who were promoted in the past are more likely to be promoted in the future. Consistent with Lazear (1992), Baker, Gibbs, and Holmstrom (1994a) report that hierarchical levels are very important to wage determination. Level dummies are the most important explanatory variables for pay data.

Jobs and Turnover

Turnover rates vary with the demographic characteristics of the underlying groups. An especially important variable in explaining turnover rates is the individual's tenure with the firm.[13] While individual characteristics may be important in explaining turnover rates, it is also possible that the characteristics of the job itself affect turnover. Thus an individual with given characteristics assigned to one particular job may have a higher probability of exit from that job than if that same individual were assigned to another job. Jobs may have lives of their own with respect to turnover rates, and the job may in fact be more important in explaining turnover than the underlying characteristics of the workers who hold it.

An additional question that comes up in the context of internal labor markets relates to the transition from one job to another. While there has been a great deal of study of mobility between firms, there has been very

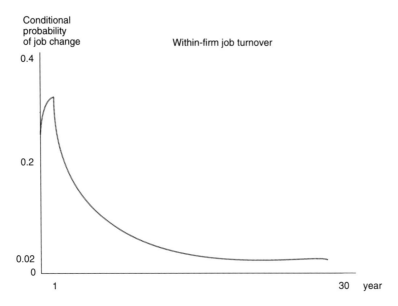

Figure 7.1

little study of mobility within firms from one job to another. Promotions, demotions, and lateral transfers are known to exist and to be pervasive, but very little is known about their patterns within firms and how those patterns vary with the characteristics of the firm itself.

In my large firm data set I found that the within-firm turnover rate from job to job resembles between-firm turnover rates, at least as those rates relate to job tenure. Specifically the pattern is as shown in figure 7.1. The probability that a worker who has started his job this year will move to another job within the firm is quite high; it is above 20 percent. By the time the worker has been with the firm for five years, the probability of a job change within that year to another job within the firm has fallen to 2 percent. It then remains at or around 2 percent throughout the worker's entire lifetime. This pattern is very similar to the one observed for inter-firm mobility. Workers are much more likely to leave their current firm for another firm during the first couple of years on the job. After they have been with the firm for a considerable amount of time, the chances that they will move to another firm are extremely low. Note that the probability of a job change within the firm goes up slightly at the outset. The probability of a job move is higher with one year of job tenure than it is with zero years of job tenure. But from then on the conditional probability of a job change declines until it levels off after about five years. The initial positively sloped section probably reflects some learning that takes place during the first year.

Since the pattern of within-firm mobility is so similar to that of between-firm mobility, there is some likelihood that the forces that affect interfirm mobility are similar to those that affect within-firm mobility. One can imagine, for instance, that if a large firm were thought of as a collection of very small firms, intrafirm mobility within the large firm might simply be analogous to the kind of sorting that takes place among small firms through interfirm mobility. Thus moving from one department to another in a large firm does not show up as interfirm mobility, but it might be equivalent to moving from one small firm to another.

Beyond the general pattern of intrafirm mobility, some interesting specific points can be made. All jobs do not have the same "export rate," defined as the rate at which individuals leave the job in a given year. Those rates can be defined as leaving to move either to another job within the firm or to another job in another firm. While there is no clear pattern, there does seem to be a tendency for low-salary workers to be more likely to experience a promotion than high-salary workers. In other words, the probability of promotion is higher for low-level workers than it is for high-level workers. While this seems like it would be true almost trivially, it does not follow automatically. High-salary workers are not necessarily workers at the top of a hierarchical structure. For example, in many organizations highly paid sales people make much more than management types who are, in theory, at higher levels and fewer in numbers. Second, there is no necessary reason why the shape of the firm's job pyramid is narrow at the top and wide at the bottom. At least in theory, it could go the other way. There might be a large number of higher-paid, higher-trained individuals and very few lower-trained, lower-paid individuals in an organization. For example, a professional corporation with many engineers may have very few secretaries if the firm is engaged in research and development. Third, confounding any promotion rates are individuals who are hired from the outside. Thus high-salaried workers could be promoted at a more rapid rate than low-salaried workers simply because all the intermediate positions in the firm are filled from the outside, whereas those at the very top of the firm are filled from within. A more detailed analysis of the data can determine which factors are at play in determining the lower promotion rates among higher-salaried workers. Each question, taken by itself, is interesting and worthy of study. Very little is known in this area, and there is much to learn.

Ports of Entry

The internal labor market literature argues that there are ports of entry in the firm. Workers have to enter the organization in particular jobs and are promoted primarily from within. Put in other terms, the "ports-of-entry" school argues that high-level jobs are closed to individuals from the outside and only low-level jobs are open.

More specifically, if the ports-of-entry view holds, then the probability of having held a job in the company may be expected to be positively related to the position of the job in the firm's hierarchy. The higher up the job, the more likely is the incumbent to have come from a previous position within the firm. In the data that I examined, there is indeed evidence that most workers enter at low-level jobs. This is because most jobs in the firm are low level, so if we simply compute the proportion of individuals who entered the firm in these low-level jobs, that proportion will be very high. A more telling statistic compares the proportion hired into a particular job with the proportion holding that job in the firm. For example, suppose that there were only two jobs in the firm and that 90 percent of workers were in one job, with 10 percent of the workers being in another job. It would not be surprising to find that 90 percent of all individuals hired from the outside were hired into the job that includes the vast majority of workers within the firm. It would be more interesting, however, if 99 percent of all workers hired from the outside landed in the large job group. Then one could conclude that workers were hired out of proportion into, say, the low-level job. In fact there is some evidence that a disproportionate share of hiring takes place in lower-level jobs, which seems to provide support for the port-of-entry view of the labor market.

While there may be some evidence that workers tend to be hired into lower levels of the firm, it is also quite clear that even high-level jobs in this firm are open to outsiders. In the firm studied, 90 percent of the jobs (not of workers) hired more than 35 percent of their workers from the outside. There appears to be plenty of chance for entry into this firm, even at the higher-level jobs.

Matching

A number of researchers have pushed the job-matching story as first articulated by Jovanovic (1979).[14] Matching models were designed to explain mobility across firms rather than within firms. But the concept of matching can also be applied to job movement within a given firm. In the same way that a worker who is a good match for a particular firm is expected to remain with that firm for a long period of time, a worker who is a good match for a particular job is expected to remain with that job for a long period of time.

Another view of labor market mobility is that job-specific skills are not particularly important. What matters most is that overall ability and movement through the firm's hierarchy reflect the search for the most able individual. That worker should and generally does end up at the top of the pyramid. Under this alternative view, workers who do best in a particular job are promoted out because their high levels of performance are most likely to reflect high levels of ability that generalize across jobs rather than a match-specific ability component that centers on jobs.

The same argument could be made for mobility between firms. There could be high-ability firms and low-ability firms where workers are sorted optimally. Some firms have technologies that are better suited to using highly able high-wage workers, whereas other firms are better suited to using less able low-wage workers.

The two models have very different implications for wage dynamics. If matching is important at the job level, then individuals who remain in the job for long periods of time are the ones best suited to and most productive in those jobs. As a result job tenure should be positively correlated with wages within the job. The ability model predicts the reverse. Individuals who have been in the job for a long period of time are essentially the lemons. The better workers tend to get promoted out. Thus new entrants to a job have higher expected ability than those who have been in the job for a long period of time. Those who remain are low ability because the top part of the distribution has been swept out. The implication of this alternative view is that wages should be negatively related to tenure within the job.

The ability to find a negative relation between wages and job tenure is reduced by institutional factors. To the extent that there is bias, it goes against the alternative view and in favor of the strict matching hypothesis. Unions and other unionlike bodies often push for a strict wage-seniority relation within jobs. Individuals who have been in jobs for long periods of time have higher wages automatically, simply as a result of moving up on the seniority scale.

In most of the data that I have looked at, I have found support for the abilities version of the model rather than the job-matching version. Other factors being equal, individuals who have been in the job for a longer period of time have lower earnings, which suggests that job matching is not important, at least within the firm. Earlier work by Medoff and Abraham (1980) established this pattern as well.

Jobs and Male-Female Wage Differentials

Job-based theories can be used to explain the pattern of male-female wage differentials. Most of the differences between men and women in the labor market are reflected in the distribution of jobs rather than in the distribution of wages within jobs. While there may be some residual wage differential within a job, for the most part women get paid less than men because they hold jobs that have lower earnings on average. Even the men in female-dominated jobs receive much less than males with similar skills holding male-dominated jobs.

The usefulness of "jobs" in understanding the data can be illustrated by the following example: Suppose that men and women have exactly the same underlying distribution of ability. Suppose further that there are only two jobs in the economy: a good job, labeled a, and the bad job, labeled b. The following fact is presented: The average ability of women in every job is higher than the average ability of men in the same job. But the average male and average female in the economy as a whole have equal ability. How can this have happened?

The answer is quite straightforward. As long as the cutoff ability level for females is higher than the cutoff ability levels for males, it will be the case that women are better in both jobs than men. To see this, consider figure 7.2. The ability density functions for men and women are shown in the top and bottom panels, respectively. The distributions are identical. Suppose that a male must have ability level greater than M in order to be selected for the good job and that the female must have ability level greater than F in order to be selected for the good job. (At this point it is unimportant why the selection criteria are different for males and females. We merely take that as given. Below an argument will be presented that suggests that there are reasons other than pure discrimination for having differential ability cutoffs.)

All men whose ability exceeds M are in job a. All men whose ability falls short of M are in job b. The average level of ability among men in job a is then given by q_m^a in figure 7.2. The average level of ability for men in job b is shown as q_m^b in figure 7.2. For women the average ability in the high-level job a is q_f^a. In the low-level job the average female has ability level q_f^b.

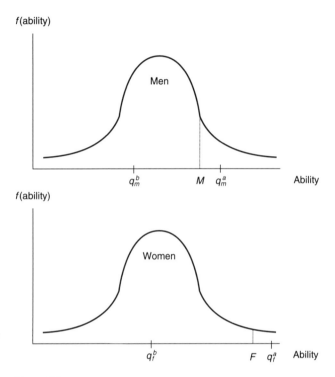

Figure 7.2

Note first that because the cutoff criterion is higher for females than males, the average level of ability among females in job *a* is higher than the average level of ability for males in job *a*. Some relatively low-ability males are able to get into job *a* because they exceed a standard that is set below the female minimum cutoff. But it is also true that the average level of ability of females in job *b* exceeds the average level of ability of males in job *b*. The reason is quite simple. High-ability females are excluded from job *a* and are thereby forced into job *b*, bringing up the average quality of females in that job. Moving a woman whose ability level is just below *F* to job *a* will drag down the average ability of females in job *a* but will also lower the average ability of females in job *b*, since that woman is the highest-ability female in job *b* but the lowest-ability female for job *a*. This example is simply a graphic illustration of the old joke told by Harvard students, in which a Harvard undergraduate moves from Harvard to Yale and brings the average up in both places. (Yale students reverse the names of the schools and tell the same joke.) In Lazear and Rosen (1990) a model is developed that allows for different jobs and explains the pattern of male-female job segregation. A slightly modified and brief description of that model is presented here.

Workers can be hired into one of two jobs, either job A or job B. Workers vary in their ability δ, and ability is given and known at the time that hiring takes place. Men and women are assumed to have the same distribution of ability in a labor market, but there is a difference. Women are assumed to be better in the nonmarket than are men.

When workers are hired into the firm in period 1, they must be placed either in job A, which is the investment job, or in job B, which is a production job that requires no investment. Output is given as follows.

$$q_1^B = \delta,$$
$$q_2^B = \delta,$$
$$q_1^A = \gamma_1 \delta,$$ (7.2)
$$q_2^A = \gamma_2 \delta,$$

where q_1^B is the output of an individual with ability δ who is sorted into job B in period 1, q_1^A is the output of an individual with ability δ who is sorted into job A in period 1 and remains there through period 2, and so forth, for the other qs. Parameters γ_1 and γ_2 are given exogenously, with $\gamma_1 < 1 < \gamma_2$. That γ_1 is less than γ_2 implies that there is learning in job A. No learning occurs in job B, and this is shown as output in the two periods being the same in job B. To take advantage of higher output in period 2, an individual must invest in period 1. Thus job A is the investment job that offers high productivity in period 2, at the cost of reduced productivity in period 1, whereas job B has no investment associated with it at all, so productivity is constant over time. In addition, to make investment worthwhile, $(1 - \gamma_1) < (\gamma_2 - 1)$.

Since workers are applying for the job, we assume that they are certain to work in period 1. The uncertainty is over whether they will continue to work in period 2. Job choice depends on the probability of working in period 2, however, because it makes no sense to invest in job skills at a cost in period 1 if the worker will not continue in period 2. Workers have an alternative use of time in period 2 that is a random variable ω. Men and women are distinguished by different distributions of ω. The distribution function of ω for men, $F_m(\omega)$, is stochastically dominated by the distribution function for women, $F_f(\omega)$:

$$F_m(\omega) > F_f(\omega) \qquad \forall \omega > 0.$$

The assumption here is that women have outside opportunities that are, on average, better than those for men. Of course this need not be specific to men or women. Any group whose outside opportunities were superior could be called women for the purposes of this model.

In competition, firms must choose a job assignment rule and a pay scale that maximize worker utility subject to a zero-profit constraint. This means that the firm must do three things. First, it must announce a wage for period 2 that induces workers to leave the firm when and only when it is efficient to do so. Second, the firm must hire efficiently. That is, it must hire individuals into their most productive activity. Third, the firm must pay a high enough wage initially to induce workers to sign on.

First, consider job assignment. A worker of ability level δ, who is hired into B, has expected output

$$\delta + \delta \int_0^\delta dF + \int_\delta^\infty \omega \, dF,$$

where F is the distribution of ω. All workers whose alternative use of time exceeds δ should not work in period 2. Instead, they should accept the alternative and receive their alternative use of time ω. Workers whose alternative use of time is less than δ work during period 2 and produce output level δ.

A worker who is assigned to job A has a lifetime expected output of

$$\delta \gamma_1 + \delta \gamma_2 \int_0^{\delta \gamma_2} dF + \int_{\delta \gamma_2}^\infty \omega \, dF.$$

In this case all workers whose alternative use of time exceeds $\gamma_2 \delta$ are separated from the firm. Note that the output levels are social output, which includes the total value of the output in period 2. That output has two components.[15] It includes the output for the worker if he remains at the firm and the output of the worker in his alternative use of time, weighted by the appropriate probabilities.

Define the difference between expected output for workers hired into job A and expected output for workers hired into job B as $D(\delta)$, given by

$$D(\delta) = -\delta(1 - \gamma_1) + \gamma_2 \delta F(\gamma_2 \delta) - \delta F(\delta) + \int_{\gamma_2 \delta}^\infty \omega dF - \int_\delta^\infty \omega dF. \qquad (7.3)$$

After rearranging terms and integrating by parts, (7.3) can be rewritten as

$$D(\delta) = -\delta(1 - \gamma_1) + \int_\delta^{\delta \gamma_2} F(\omega) d(\omega). \qquad (7.4)$$

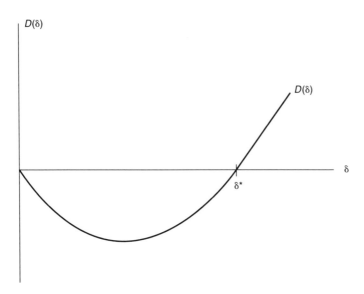

Figure 7.3

It is tedious but straightforward to show that the function $D(\delta)$ must always look as it does in figure 7.3; namely it must start at zero, decline, then rise and cross the horizontal axis at some interior $\delta = \delta^*$.

For all individuals whose ability levels fall short of δ^*, it is efficient to classify them into job B because $D(\delta)$ is negative. For all individuals whose ability levels exceed δ^*, it is efficient to classify them into job A because $D(\delta)$ exceeds δ^*. Since women's alternatives stochastically dominate those of men, the δ^* that pertains to women will be higher than the δ^* that pertains to men. Note that $D(\delta)$ in equation (7.4) depends on the distribution function. Since the distribution functions are different for men and women, the point at which $D(\delta) = 0$ will vary by gender. In this case women will have to exceed a higher level of δ^* in order to be hired into the high-level job than will men. The proof is contained in Lazear and Rosen (1990).

It is also clear from this analysis that higher-ability individuals are the ones most likely to be given the "good" job. The reason is not that they are better suited to the good job but rather that they are more likely to stay with it because they are very unlikely to have alternative opportunities that exceed those in their current organization. The direct implication is that promotions breed additional promotions.

To the extent that some of the human capital is firm specific, a worker who has already been given the opportunity to invest has increased the value of his time at the current firm, relative to his alternatives. The more investment that takes place, the bigger is the gap between his productivity at the current firm and his expected alternative use of time. This makes him less and less likely to leave. But this also means that additional investment is even more profitable. Thus individuals who have made an investment early in their career are likely to be given additional opportunities for investment.

This human capital explanation of career paths resembles tracking. Some individuals are given opportunities at young ages and continue to receive investment opportunities throughout their work lives. Others are given no opportunities and never receive additional opportunities to invest. Of course tracking of this sort is completely efficient and requires no coercion. As long as individuals know their ability levels and are charged the appropriate prices for investment, they will select these career paths voluntarily.

Discussion earlier in this chapter about how probability of promotion may be based on initial job assignment is very much in line with this model. The difference here is that initial job assignments reflect underlying characteristics; in the model presented, ability was the exogenous factor. In the earlier discussion, it was at least possible that job assignments could be made randomly but that the realization of these job assignments could lead to very different career paths. One need not rely on random assignments nor on arbitrary behavior in order to generate career paths. They are implied directly by the human capital investment model.

Returning to the issue of discrimination, note that women are less likely to get promoted than men. Since the distribution of ability for females is the same as that for males within the organization, it is less likely that a female will exceed her promotion ability level than a male because the female promotion hurdle is higher. This has nothing to do with discrimination; it merely reflects an optimal job sorting. The woman would herself choose job B over job A if her ability level fell below the female ability cutoff.

This issue also gives rise to the result that was discussed at the beginning of this section. Women will be of higher ability in every job than their male counterparts, and this occurs without any differences in the underlying structure of labor market ability and without discrimination. Women and men are assumed to have the same labor market abilities, but the sorting is different because alternative uses of time are assumed to be better for women.

8   Evaluation

Firms devote many resources to a variety of types of evaluation. There is
a large industry in consulting that focuses exclusively on evaluating actions taken by the firm and the personnel in it. There are primarily two
kinds of evaluation that are of interest in the current context. First, jobs are
evaluated to determine their importance in the firm, the need for them and
the compensation that should be attached to them. Second, individuals
who hold those jobs are evaluated so that their performance can be rewarded appropriately. A significant amount of attention has already been
paid to job evaluation, although most of it was in the context of other
topics. Performance evaluation, which is far more pervasive, has been the
cornerstone for much of the variable pay discussions. But up to this point,
we have simply assumed that job evaluation of some type occurs, without
being explicit on how the evaluation is actually done. Before discussing
performance evaluation, we turn first to job evaluation for some additional
detail.

Job Evaluation

Job evaluation has already been discussed in the context of index numbers.
The level of sophistication on job evaluation is incredibly low in the personnel literature. Not only are the deep and fundamental questions involving statistical identification ignored, but much more basic problems
are simply overlooked. For example, one text, which discusses the assignments of weights to various factors in job evaluation,[1] suggests the following as a possible approach: Simply assign points to each factor and add
the points to get a ranking of jobs. Second, rank jobs overall without
reference to individual factors. Then check to see if the correlation between the two methods is the same. At best, all this does is validate the
consistency of the rankings. It does not say that they are right.

Table 8.1
Ambiguity of job evaluation

		Scale 1	Scale 2
Scale 1:	Responsibility	1–100	
	Skill	1–10	
Scale 2:	Responsibility	1–10	
	Skill	1–100	
School bus driver	Responsibility	100	10
	Skill	1	1
	Total	101	11
Professional golfer	Responsibility	1	1
	Skill	10	100
	Total	11	101

There are at least two sources of ambiguity in job evaluation. The first is that different evaluators may index jobs in different ways because of their subjective opinions. Second, the scaling of indexes introduces another source of arbitrariness. Let us focus on the second problem now.

Consider the two scales as shown in table 8.1. Scale 1 indexes the responsibility associated with a job between 1 and 100 points and the skill associated with a job between 1 and 10 points. Scale 2 indexes responsibility as between 1 and 10 and skill as between 1 and 100. Now consider two jobs: school bus driver and professional golfer. The school bus driver, who has in his hands the lives of many small children, has a high degree of responsibility in his job. On the other hand, the skill associated with driving a school bus is not all that great. Most people who know how to drive can learn to drive a bus very quickly and most evaluators would attribute a low skill level to this job. A professional golfer, on the other hand, has virtually no responsibility associated with the job. The cost associated with the failures of a professional golfer are borne almost exclusively by himself and perhaps by his family; there are no larger implications for society. But few would disagree that the skill required to perform successfully in professional golf is extremely high. Thus let us give highest rankings to golfers on skill but lowest rankings on responsibility, and highest rankings to school bus drivers on responsibility but lowest rankings on skill. Table 8.1 shows that if scale 1 is used, the total number of points associated with the bus driver's job is 101 and the total number of points associated with the professional golfer's job is 11. If scale 2 is used, the total number of points associated with the bus driver's job is 11 and the total number of points associated with the professional golfer's job is 101. If compensation were to be based on these point scales, it is quite clear that the results would depend almost entirely on the choice of scale.

Choosing a scale is not a clear-cut activity. Economists might attempt to set up scales by using regressions, which list responsibility and skills as independent (right-hand side) variables and the market wage as the dependent variable. The coefficient obtained from the regressions would then be the weights given to each of the factors. Doing so is somewhat more scientific than the trial-and-error approach suggested by personnel texts, but it still suffers from all the inherent problems of index number theory and variable definition problems.

In theory there is a way to resolve this issue of scaling. Consider the wage regression

$$\text{Wage} = \alpha + \beta(\text{skill}) + \gamma(\text{responsibility}). \tag{8.1}$$

Suppose for the moment that skill is a variable that lends itself readily to measurement and that the same is true for the responsibility variable. Market data can be collected on a cross section of jobs where information on wage scale and responsibility are all available. The regression of (8.1) can be run to obtain estimates of coefficient β, α, and γ. It is then quite straightforward to create a range for skill and responsibility.

Let skill, as it is currently measured, vary between, say, 0 and 17. These numbers are arbitrary because any rescaling of skill will simply alter proportionately the estimated coefficient β. Suppose that responsibility, as measured, varies between 20 and 40. Suppose further that β is estimated to be 0.2 and that γ is estimated to be 0.1. Then the index for skill in dollars is unambiguous and ranges between 0 and 3.4. The index for responsibility is also unambiguous and ranges between 2 and 4. Furthermore these have the interpretation of dollar increases in wages, so a job that has a skill requirement of 40 pays $2 more per hour than a job with a skill requirement of 20. Similarly a job that has a skill requirement of 17 pays $3.40 more than a job that has a skill requirement of 0.

Even if this regression can be run, and the required data are readily available, there are still some problems associated with the technique. First, as with all regressions, functional form may be an important issue. But this is a minor problem that can be resolved by sufficiently rich data. Second, objectivity of the indexes skill and responsibility cannot always be guaranteed. It was assumed that all individuals would rank different jobs in the same way, with respect to skill and responsibility. But in reality that assumption is far from valid. When workers and managers are asked to rank jobs on a variety of characteristics, the rankings differ significantly across evaluators, and the evaluators are biased. For example, there is a tendency for women to rank jobs that are female dominated more highly than males do, and vice versa.[2]

While the scaling of skills and of responsibility are of no consequence in the regression, because the estimated coefficients adjust appropriately, the subjectivity of the evaluator is a significant problem. The problem is not unique to this particular setting, but it is more pronounced in this context. When survey administrators collect data on wages, levels of schooling, and so forth, in large cross section or panel data sets, the questions being asked tend to have much more objective answers than the ones that are being discussed here. To the extent that subjectivity is going to be a problem, it is likely to be very important in the current context.

Even if the issues of objectivity are resolved, there remains the question of interpretation raised by the identification problem. The regression in (8.1) may fit the market data, but that regression does not provide information about the trade-offs that any *given* firm or its workers are willing to make. Thus changing compensation on the basis of the regression in (8.1) could end up disrupting the entire work force and inducing large quits or layoffs.

Finally, job evaluation tends to focus on job characteristics and to ignore the characteristics of the incumbents. Since there is a great deal of variation in worker characteristics within any given job, an additional factor is wage variation within a job. Job evaluation focuses only on between-job wage variation and ignores differences in compensation that go to individuals within a given job category. But within-job variation may be as important or more important than that between different job categories. Generally practitioners who engage in job evaluation think about within-job wage variation almost as an afterthought. First, job wage scales are set up based on something like the methodology used in table 8.1 to anchor particular jobs to particular wage levels. Then an arbitrary, and usually quite subjective, scale is imposed to allow variation within the job. Despite all the "science" that is focused on between-job wage variation, very little is focused on within-job wage variation. Human capital and other variables are taken into account only insofar as they affect the average characteristics of incumbents in a particular job.

Performance Appraisal

Very little has been said about performance appraisal, so I turn to that topic now. Performance appraisal is also a very important aspect of personnel management. Most of us, as academics, get involved with performance evaluation a few times a year when we determine the fates of our junior colleagues who are up for promotion. But the theory on which performance appraisal is based is very loose at best. In what follows, I discuss the timing of appraisals, the frequency of appraisals, and how appraisals vary with the characteristics of jobs.

Reinforcement of workers through evaluation and raises is not completely dissimilar from psychologists' notion of reinforcement of laboratory animals in a behavioral setting. Pigeons, rats, dogs, and other animals can be induced to behave in particular ways by reinforcing or punishing their behavior. For example, pigeons can be induced to peck on a disk by issuing a pellet of food every time the disk is pecked. By altering the schedule of reinforcement, different behavioral responses can be initiated. Furthermore the response can be "extinguished" by eliminating or reducing to a sufficiently low frequency the reinforcement associated with the behavior.[3] Worker behavior, which is rewarded by the weekly paycheck, is in some respects like the rewards given to laboratory animals, but there are two major differences.

First, economists think about the problem somewhat differently from the way psychologists do. An economist models the worker's response to evaluation and reinforcement as a direct result of optimizing behavior. Thus, as economists, it is important to provide a structure in which workers maximize utility and firms maximize profits.

Second, the structure that evolves must be compatible with markets. Laboratory animals are slaves to their experimenters, but workers are not slaves to their employers. Workers who do not like the environment in which they work can always leave and move to another firm. A disgruntled laboratory animal has no such option. Thus we model evaluation in a maximizing and competitive framework where workers have alternatives.[4]

The issue to be addressed is the frequency with which workers are evaluated and rewarded. How often should an employee be told that he performed well on the job? In the academic market, serious evaluations occur only a couple of times during the worker's entire work life, coming at promotion and tenure decisions. In other jobs, evaluation is more frequent. Also, when does the evaluation occur? Should most of it happen early in the career, late in the career, or should it occur uniformly throughout the work life?

To model this, suppose that a worker produces some base level of output equal to zero with probability $1 - P$. With some probability P, he is more productive in the firm, in which case he produces output level of 1.

The worker lives two periods and can move to another firm at the end of the first period, where he will receive W. It costs a firm τ to determine whether the worker is producing 0 or 1.

Consider two different evaluation and payment schemes. In one scheme the worker is evaluated once and only once during his career. Since the labor market is competitive, the worker receives his marginal product, minus the cost of evaluation. Low evaluation ratings and corresponding low pay may induce the worker to leave. In the second scheme the worker is never evaluated and stays with the firm during the entire work life. There is no reduction in salary for evaluation costs, but unproductive workers sometimes remain with the firm even if they are more productive elsewhere.

The scenario here is virtually identical to the one described in chapter 2, when the choice was between paying a salary or piece rate. In the case of paying a piece rate, workers are measured and compensated accordingly. In the case of paying a salary, workers were simply given the average wage for the firm. That model can be extended to derive a number of implications.

First, the value of frequent evaluation goes up as the value of the worker's alternatives rise. The more valuable is the job switch, the more important is it to evaluate workers to provide them with the information that enables them to take advantage of higher productivity opportunities. Probationary periods serve the worker's interest because they provide information on which the worker can act. If workers are not given this information, then they do not switch jobs optimally, and the average output of the firm is correspondingly lower. As a result workers' wages will be lower. For a sufficiently low cost of measurement, it pays to provide information early so that the worker can stay at the job, or move to a more productive use of his time. It is also quite straightforward to show that as the probability of success rises, infrequent evaluation becomes optimal. If most workers are better suited to this firm than they are to other firms, then it is wasteful to bear measurement costs for all, just to sort out a few unproductive workers.

To restate and expand upon some of the implications from chapter 2, recall the condition that determined whether a worker was paid a piece rate or a salary. He was paid a piece rate iff, as in (2.9),

$$wF(w) - \int_{q_{\min}}^{w} qf(q)\,dq > \frac{\tau}{1 - \lambda}.$$

Recall that w is the worker's alternative use of time and that $f(q)$ is the density function of output in the worker's current firm. The cost of measurement is given by τ, and the proportion of the work life spent measuring the worker is λ.

The large costs of measurement (a high value of τ) probably account for the infrequency of evaluation in academe. The output of most academics is difficult to define, let alone observe, and comparisons are often highly subjective. Indeed the inability to assess output in an absolute manner is one of the arguments for thinking about academic promotions as fitting the tournament structure.

Workers with output that is easily observed should be evaluated frequently and should experience frequent changes in their compensation to reflect changing output. Thus a secretary should be evaluated more frequently than his boss, because a boss's output is much more difficult to characterize. Low-wage individuals with well-defined tasks are evaluated more frequently, not because of some inherent character flaw that is prevalent among less skilled workers but rather because the information about output is cheaper to come by for low-wage workers.

Also recall that the left-hand side of (2.9) is increasing in w. For a given density function $f(q)$, a higher value of w implies that the probability of success in the firm is lower. Success here means that output in the current job exceeds the value of the alternative use of time w. So, as the value of alternatives rises, the probability of achieving relative success falls.

In the business world, activities where failure is common relative to the alternatives should be evaluated often. Thus investment bankers and consultants should be assessed on a frequent basis. Relatively few individuals in those fields have productivity that exceeds that of their alternative use of time. This is not so much because the value of their alternatives is high but because very few people have the talent to make it in investment banking or consulting. Frequent evaluation weeds most individuals out. At the other extreme are jobs like bank tellers in which performance is not likely to vary a great deal. Once hired and past a probationary period, most bank tellers are likely to find their output to be quite stable over their lifetimes. As a result frequent evaluation has little value to the bank or to the teller.

Even within academe the same implications hold. At schools where the likelihood of tenure is high because alternatives are relatively poor, evaluation should be infrequent. At schools where tenure probabilities are very low, evaluation should be more frequent and more important.

As mentioned in an earlier chapter, evaluation should be more frequent at the beginning of a worker's career than at the end. The value of evaluation is greatest when it comes at the time when much can be gained by acting on the information.[5] It is quite straightforward to prove this conjecture by extending the analysis of chapter 2 from a two-period to a three-period context. Instead of having probation and then the rest of the worker's lifetime, there can be two probationary periods. It is trivial to show that as long as measurement costs are the same regardless of when the measurement is undertaken, it always pays to undertake measurement and evaluation early. If a worker is to be evaluated, say, ten times over the career, then a disproportionate amount of evaluation should occur during the first few years on the job. This surely fits the pattern in academe, where most serious evaluation is done early. It also tends to fit the pattern in industry, where workers are weeded out within the first few months on the job. Doctoral students take their exams very early in the program so that their likelihood of success can be ascertained quickly. It makes no sense to induce an individual to invest many years in occupation-specific skills if he is better suited to another activity.

Earlier references were made to the behavioral psychology literature where laboratory animals are induced to behave in a particular way by a specific reinforcement schedule. Ferster and Skinner (1957) spend much of their time estimating the effects of fixed and variable reinforcement schedules. A variable reinforcement schedule is one that is like a mixed strategy. With a variable reinforcement scheme, sometimes when a pigeon pecks at a lever, the machine rewards the bird with a pellet of food. But sometimes the peck does not result in a pellet of food. If the pattern is obvious to the pigeon—for example, a pellet is received every two pecks—then the response extinguishes very quickly after the machine has stopped delivering pellets. But if the payment is simply probabilistic, so that one-half the time, on average, the pigeon receives food after pecking the lever, the pigeon will continue to peck the lever for a longer period of time after the machine has stopped rewarding.

Similarly variable reward, or noise in the evaluation process, makes inference more difficult for a worker. Thus scrambling the signal that a worker receives on evaluation is more likely to induce the worker to stay at the current firm.

It might appear that a profit-maximizing firm would like to confuse workers strategically so that they would stay on at low wages, even when leaving is preferable. But here the difference between workers and laboratory animals is crucial. Since workers must be hired in a competitive environment, a firm that scrambles evaluation signals is forced to pay higher average wages to workers when hiring them. It is easy to show that the additional amount paid to workers always exceeds the value to the firm of keeping the workers on.

The result is obvious at one level. There are no externalities, so efficient behavior must be elicited by the competitive equilibrium. Efficient behavior requires that firms provide appropriate information to their workers. But key to this result is that a firm's reputation perfectly reflects any scrambling behavior in which the firm engages.

Formally, recall that the probability that a worker is productive at a firm is P, where productivity is defined as the ability to produce one unit of output. If the worker is unproductive, he produces zero units of output. Firms can send a scrambled signal to their workers after the first period. Let us consider the following kind of scrambling. When a firm scrambles, it lies to a productive worker at the end of period 1, telling him that he was not productive in the past and will not be paid for that period. Along with the message are some encouraging words about the likelihood of payment in the future. The worker understands that the failure to be paid in the first period may be a reflection of a true failure on the worker's part or may simply reflect the firm's desire to confuse its work force so as to induce productive workers to stay at the firm, even when pay is low.[6] Since the firm is scrambling S of the time, the Bayesian inference problem is straightforward. The relevant probabilities are given in (8.2):

$$\text{Prob(pay in period 1)} = (1 - S)P, \tag{8.2a}$$

$$\text{Prob(no pay in period 1)} = SP + 1 - P, \tag{8.2b}$$

$$\text{Prob(pay in 2 | pay in 1)} = 1. \tag{8.2c}$$

Given the probabilities in (8.2), the conditional probability of pay in period 2, given that the worker was told that he was a low-quality worker and not paid in period 1, is

$$\text{Prob(pay in 2 | no pay in 1)} = \frac{SP}{SP + 1 - P}. \tag{8.3}$$

The worker has an alternative wage offer w, so the worker stays if

$$w < \frac{R_S SP}{SP + 1 - P}, \tag{8.4}$$

where R_S is the per-period wage in an environment where firms scramble the signal.

Scrambling induces two kinds of mistakes. First, if R_S and S are sufficiently high, then all workers will stay because those who are not paid in period 1 still believe that the probability of receiving income in period 2 is high enough to warrant staying. This is analogous to the pigeon continuing to peck at the lever that has stopped rewarding him. It results in unproductive workers inefficiently staying at the firm. Second, for sufficiently low values of S and R_S, all workers who are not paid in period 1 quit. This means that some who are productive inefficiently leave the firm and reduce overall output.

Obviously both kinds of errors cannot take place. Either S and R_S are sufficiently high that workers remain with the firm even when no pay is given, or S and R_S are sufficiently low that all unpaid workers switch. Let us consider a case where S and R_s are sufficiently high to retain all workers, even after a poor first-period evaluation. The result of course is that firms receive higher profits for any *given* salary. Firms that scramble with probability S receive

$$\Pi_S = 2P - P(1 - S)R_S - PR_S - \tau, \tag{8.5}$$

where τ is the cost of measurement. The expected output of workers is $2P - \tau$, and the second and third terms reflect the amount of salary that workers receive over the two periods.

If the world consisted of firms that always told the truth, then profits at those firms would be

$$\Pi_T = 2P(1 - R_T) - \tau, \tag{8.6}$$

where Π_T is the profit for firms telling the truth and R_T is the wage rate paid by those firms. The difference between (8.5) and (8.6) is given by

$$\Pi_S - \Pi_T = PR_S(S - 2) + 2PR_T. \tag{8.7}$$

Now consider two towns. In one town, firms scramble. In the other town, they do not. The worker will be indifferent between working the two towns when

$$PR_S(2 - S) = 2PR_T + (1 - P)W.$$

The left-hand side is the expected wage over two periods at a firm that scrambles. The right-hand side is the expected wage at a firm that reveals information truthfully. This expression can be rewritten as

$$R_T = \frac{R_S(2 - S)}{2} - \frac{(1 - P)W}{2P}. \tag{8.8}$$

To get workers to work in the town where scrambling occurs, (8.8) must be satisfied. Substitution of (8.8) into (8.7) yields

$$\Pi_S - \Pi_T = -(1 - P)W,$$

which is negative. The profit of firms in the truth-telling town is always higher than the profits of those in the scrambling town. Equilibrium is characterized by truth-telling firms.

While it is true that firms were able to induce their workers to stay on by scrambling the signal, the cost of doing so was a higher wage rate, which in equilibrium always exceeds the additional profit obtained. That is, if R_T were equal to R_S, the right-hand side of (8.6) would always be positive. But $R_S > R_T$ because firms that do not provide trustworthy information in period 1 must pay higher wages to their workers, which reduces profits below the truth-telling strategy.

A similar analysis shows that scrambling, which results in the departure of all first-period workers, is also unprofitable. It does not matter whether the error is of one type or another. When it is possible to eliminate error costlessly, a competitive environment will always induce the truth to be told.

Are evaluations always honest? This depends on the ability of a firm's reputation to catch up with it. If a firm can lie to its workers without bearing the costs, then there are circumstances under which it will pay the firm to lie. This amounts to allowing firms that scramble to pay R_T rather than R_S. But as long as a firm's evaluation policy is known to workers at the time of hire, the firm has to behave in an honest fashion, and R_S will exceed R_T.

The frequency and timing of evaluations have implications for areas outside the labor economics sphere. Loan repayment schedules and collateral requirements can be analyzed in the same way as evaluations can. Similarly scheduling of bill payments is closely related to the issue of worker evaluation and reward. Creditors are given information when loans are paid off continuously. The installments provide information about whether the borrower is likely to continue to pay back the loan. More important, to the extent that collateral is available through repossession, nonpayment of an installment signals to the creditor that the borrower is a bad risk at a time when repossession of collateral still has value. But just as scrambling a signal requires that firms pay something to the workers, loans that give creditors the right to repossess require that interest rates be set lower in return for the option. Whether loans are installment loans with collateral or zero coupon loans without collateral depends on the relative value of the collateral to the borrower and lender.[7]

In addition to a discussion of the timing of evaluations, it is interesting to consider the substance of evaluation. What factors should be evaluated?

Much has already been said earlier that has direct bearing on performance evaluation. We restate some of those points here.

First, the firm must decide whether it is to evaluate a worker on his input or on his output. Measurement costs are probably most important here. When it is difficult to judge output or when output is affected in large part by random events over which the worker has little control (and when the worker is more risk averse than the firm), the evaluation should be based on input rather than output. Having made a good effort and put in long hours might be a better indicator of performance than a very poor measure of an individual's output.

Second, when output measures are available, the output that is relevant is the present value of the profit stream. All the standard issues that relate to short-run versus long-run goals are relevant here. A worker who sacrifices profitable long-run opportunities to raise current earnings should not be evaluated as highly as one who makes the appropriate trade-offs. While sounding somewhat trite, I believe this is less obvious than it appears. Individuals who set up internal evaluation schemes may be adept at measuring outcomes but less well qualified to define the desired outcomes. One need only look at the incentive schemes used in state enterprises in command economies to know that it is not obvious that firms know to focus on profit, rather than quantity.

Third, almost by definition, evaluation is based on relative rather than absolute comparisons. It is difficult to know what is good without comparing it to something. But comparisons can be made to some "absolute" standard that adjusts over time as a function of normed output. At a point in time such an evaluation would appear to be based on absolute rather than relative performance because all workers in the group could score above or all could score below the standard. Evaluations based on relative comparisons (not standards) are therefore most useful when there is a great deal of temporal variation and when the variation affects all workers in the group in a similar way. Relative evaluation differences out these common noise effects.

Fourth, output-based evaluation must recognize the difference between quantity and quality. This is really just a special case of the second point that present value of profit be the sole criterion. But the worker should be rewarded for adopting the same trade-off between quality and quantity as the consumer makes in his willingness to pay for a higher-quality unit. Evaluation should therefore be based on the market trade-off in money of quality for quantity.

9   Institutions

This chapter is devoted exclusively to institutions. The word "institution" is somewhat overused in economics. I define institutions as those constraints, either formal or informal, that operate outside the price system. Institutions may arise because of efficiency considerations, but the institutions themselves manipulate behavior without resorting to standard price mechanisms. The most important institutions, as far as the labor market is concerned, are the legal environment and the formal structure of industrial relations, primarily unions and other negotiating bodies. While the legal environment and unions may have effects on prices and wages, they impose constraints that often work outside the price system. For example, laws that prohibit certain kinds of behavior do not generally rely on prices to affect behavior. Employers may be required to "negotiate with workers in good faith." It is conceivable that the competitive market could establish prices and wages such that firms that did not negotiate with workers in good faith were required to pay higher wages. Then the price system would replace the legal structure and institutions would not be necessary to bring this behavior about. But the legal structure is an alternative to a competitive market mechanism.

Even here there is some ambiguity. The legal structure could set up a system of prices, such as fines, that simply charge the firm for particular kinds of behavior and allow the firm to decide whether to engage in it or not. The legal system would be using a pricing mechanism, but it would still be, by my definition, an institution because it does not evolve automatically through market forces that determine prices.

In addition to the legal environment and trade unions, the definition of institutions includes more informal aspects of social pressure that affect firm-worker relations. The discussion can be most instructive by laying out some specific examples.

Tenure

One specific institution, namely mandatory retirement, has already been discussed in the context of work life incentive schedules. There are other, related, institutions that deserve mention as well.

Many organizations engage in granting explicit or implicit tenure. Both European and American academic institutions, on the whole, give tenure to individuals who have achieved a certain status within the university. In Europe, particularly in France, Italy, and Spain, workers in private industry also have job tenure, although tenure is not formally granted. In part, the patterns we observe in European firms are a result of government severance pay requirements.[1] When governments mandate that laid-off workers must be given severance pay, the cost of terminating the workers rises. This also implies of course that employers will be much more cautious about hiring, and the overall effect on employment may actually be negative.[2]

Tenure is an interesting institution, and it is important to be able to explain its existence. Two theories have surfaced. One view says that tenure comes about after a worker has been with a firm for a long enough period of time. At this point enough positive signals on the worker's productivity have been received so that the firm would not sever the worker's employment under any circumstances.[3] This is essentially an extension of the job-matching story of Jovanovic (1979). After a string of sufficiently positive signals has been received, the optimal employment rule is to retain the worker, irrespective of future negative signals.

An alternative view is more strategic and emphasizes the importance of relative performance in the firm. Carmichael (1988) has argued that when compensation is relative, and when the individuals who do the hiring are to be in the same pool with those hired, there is an incentive to hire people strategically.[4] Incumbents do not want competition from good outsiders, and so they tend to hire lower-quality people than would otherwise be optimal for the firm. A way to avoid this problem is to grant tenure to the current incumbents, especially to those incumbents who have the power to determine hiring.[5] By doing this, incumbents are somewhat insulated from competition from new hires.[6]

The theory works well to explain the difference between academic and other jobs because academicians have control over hiring of their junior colleagues. It also fits in law firms and accounting firms quite well. Partners are granted tenure, and those partners also have control over hiring decisions made by others. But in many wage and salary firms, individuals who have no control over hiring and no effect on evaluation of their peers are still granted tenure explicitly. Furthermore it is difficult to justify international differences in tenure behavior by appealing to this explanation. Still it is clear that as a personnel matter, granting tenure will affect the incentives of incumbents, not only with respect to effort but also with respect to their views of others in the firm.

Monopsony and Dishonesty

Firms have incentives to be somewhat dishonest with their workers, and institutions have arisen to take care of this particular problem. The general phenomenon occurs when firms are paying workers more than they could receive at their alternative jobs. Under these circumstances firms have an incentive to lie to workers about their productivity in an attempt to keep workers around even at wages that fall short of their marginal product. This type of dishonesty creates distortions in the labor market on a number of margins.[7] Specifically, when firms underreport a worker's value and use this to underpay a worker, his incentive to leave the firm increases, even when it would be efficient for him to stay. Before discussing the institutions that may be able to deal with this problem, let us set up the formal structure.

Suppose that the true value of a worker is V. Let the firm report that his value is $\hat{V}$. The worker's alternative use of time is $\hat{W}$, but the firm does not know $\hat{W}$ precisely. Instead, it knows that $\hat{W}$ has density function $f(\hat{W})$.

The firm pays the worker the reported value, $\hat{V}$. But if $\hat{V} < \hat{W}$, the worker leaves.[8] Thus the firm's problem is

$$\underset{\hat{V}}{\text{Max}}\ (V - \hat{V})F(\hat{V}).$$ (9.1)

On each worker kept, the firm earns rent equal to $V - \hat{V}$. For any $\hat{W}$ the probability that a worker stays is the probability that $\hat{V} > \hat{W}$ or $F(\hat{V})$. The first-order condition is

$$(V - \hat{V})f(\hat{V}) - F(\hat{V}) = 0,$$

or

$$\hat{V} = V - \frac{F(\hat{V})}{f(\hat{V})}.$$ (9.2)

Equation (9.2) says that a firm will always announce a productivity and wage level that is below true productivity. It pays to take a chance on losing the worker because no rents are earned if the wage is set as high as true productivity. Every firm acts as an ex post monopsonist. The behavior described in equation (9.2) creates a clear inefficiency. There are values V, w, and $\hat{V}$ such that workers will be induced to leave when they should otherwise stay. For example, if

$$\hat{V} < \hat{W} < V$$

or

$$V - \frac{F(\hat{V})}{f(V)} < \hat{W} < V$$

holds, then the worker will leave because his alternative wage exceeds the wage he is receiving at the current firm. Yet he should stay because his alternative wage falls short of his marginal product in the current firm.

Up-or-Out

Up-or-out is another labor market institution that can help deal with dishonest behavior by firms. It is frequently combined with tenure. Under up-or-out there is an evaluation point when a worker's performance is judged. If it is found to be satisfactory, he is promoted. If it is found to be unsatisfactory, he is dismissed. There is no middle ground. Workers are not retained at lower wages when they fail their performance evaluation. This is somewhat puzzling, since there should be some conditions under which the firm should be willing keep the worker.

Kahn and Huberman (1988) explain up-or-out as a way to help the firm commit to a strategy. If workers can be told that their performance is unsatisfactory and that their wages are going to be lower as a result, then firms have an incentive to lie to workers by always reducing the reported productivity below its true level, as in (9.2). But if firms are forced to fire workers that they rate as poor, then the firm's incentives are different. Lying about a worker's productivity may do no good and can actually reduce the firm's profit. With up-or-out, lying causes the firm to lose workers that it would like to keep. Thus committing to a strategy of up-or-out is a way to enforce truth telling. This can be presented more rigorously using the framework of the model.

Suppose that V can take on one of two values:

$V = V_H$ with probability P,

$V = V_L$ with probability $1 - P$.

The firm can report $\hat{V} = \{V_H, V_L\}$, but now there is an up-or-out constraint: If V_L is reported, the firm must terminate the worker. The wage for workers who are kept is w, where $V_L < w < V_H$, and it is determined by bargaining power, which is fixed in advance as a feature of the up-or-out contract.

Workers have alternative wage $\hat{w}$, where $V_L < \hat{w} < V_H$. If the firm observes that a worker's output is V_L, it will report V_L and terminate the worker. It clearly does not pay to keep a worker with $V < w$, and all workers with $V = V_L$ would receive $w > V$, since $w > V_L$.

If the firm observes that a worker's output is V_H, it has a choice. The firm can report V_H and pay w. The rent that the firm earns is then $V_H - w > 0$. Alternatively, the firm can report V_L. But doing so requires termination by the up-or-out rules. The rent is then zero. The firm is better off telling the truth.

Up-or-out creates incentives that induce the firm to tell the truth. While the firm would like to lie about output and pay a lower wage, it is precluded from doing so by the up-or-out contract. This contract causes the firm to tell the truth, and in this case, the contract also results in efficient separation. The worker leaves the firm whenever his output is V_L, which falls short of the alternative use of time, and is kept whenever output is V_H, which exceeds the alternative use of time. Thus efficiency is guaranteed.

The example of two states is more than a mere convenience. When the distribution of V is continuous, as it was in equations (9.1) and (9.2), some additional restrictions must be imposed to make the case for up-or-out contracts. Still the general principle that forcing a firm to terminate any worker whom the firm reports to be low quality is a scheme that can induce firms to tell the truth.

Legal Constraints in the Labor Market

Firms face many constraints that are imposed on them by the legal system. In this section one point is emphasized: In determining a firm's posture with respect to labor regulations, relative comparisons among firms may be more important than absolute valuations. The point is best illustrated through two examples.

First, consider minimum wage legislation. It is generally thought that firms oppose minimum wage legislation because minimum wages have the effect of raising the compensation that they pay to their work force. The following example points out cases where firms may actually favor minimum wage legislation.

Table 9.1
Relative costs of minimum wage

	Volvo	Saab
Before minimum		
Labor 500 hours	$5,000	$2,500
Capital	$5,000	$7,500
Cost per car	$10,000	$10,000
After minimum		
Labor 500 hours	$6,000	$3,000
Capital	$5,000	$7,500
Cost per car	$11,000	$10,500

Consider two firms that produce automobiles, say, Volvo and Saab. In order to produce one Volvo, 500 hours of labor are used, combined with $5,000 worth of capital. To produce one Saab, 250 hours of labor are used, and this is combined with $7,500 worth of capital. This is shown as the top panel of table 9.1.

Suppose that the wage is $10 per hour. Then the cost of producing a Volvo and the cost of producing a Saab are identical. Labor costs $5,000 at Volvo and $2,500 at Saab, but when combined with capital, cost per car is $10,000. Now let the minimum wage rise from $10 to $12 per hour. The cost of producing a Saab rises from $10,000 to $10,500. This is what generally leads people to think that firms will oppose minimum wages. However, with Bertrand competition, the price of the Volvo has gone from $10,000 to $11,000 because Volvos are relatively labor intensive.

If Saab's only competition in the world were Volvo, then Saab would surely favor an increase in the minimum wage, which would affect Volvo's position adversely. Because relative costs rather than absolute costs matter in a market environment, firms will favor increases in costs of labor for labor-intensive firms.[9]

The point is general and relates to any labor cost increases. Taxes or restrictions that affect labor-intensive firms more than they do capital-intensive firms will be favored by the relatively capital-intensive firms. As long as one firm's costs go up by less than the cost of its rivals, it benefits in a competitive market environment. It is the firm's relative position, rather than its absolute costs that matter, since its ability to attract customers depends not only on the price that it charges but also on the price that its rivals can charge. When products are sufficiently close substitutes and when one producer is only a portion of the market, that producer will benefit by seeing costs rise, so long as rivals' costs rise by more.

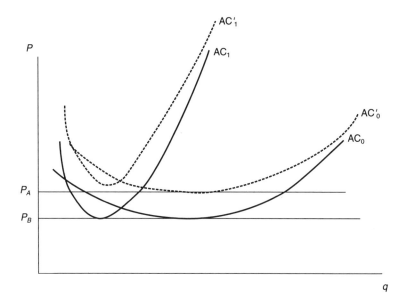

Figure 9.1

A second example comes from coal mining legislation passed about twenty years ago in the United States. A large mining accident induced Congress to initiate the Coal Mine Health and Safety Act,[10] which required mines in the United States to meet certain safety standards, necessitating the installation of safety equipment. The act was favored by western states and opposed by eastern states. The reason is quite simple.

In eastern states, mines are typically small and underground. In western states, the mines are large strip mines. A given fixed cost imposed on a large strip mine is amortized over a larger number of output units than the same fixed cost imposed on a small shaft mine. Shaft mines' costs rose by more as a result of this legislation than strip mines' costs. Because of transportation costs, most coal in the United States is domestic. Raising the costs of shaft-mined coal relative to strip-mined coal placed strip miners at a relative, although not at an absolute, advantage.

The situation is illustrated by figure 9.1. AC_0 is the average cost for strip mines, and AC_1 is the average cost for shaft mines before the legislation is passed. P_B is the price before the legislation and lies at the minimum of the average costs for both kinds of mines. Initially a long-run equilibrium was established where both types of mines were able to produce competitively in the pre-legislation environment.

Now legislation is passed that raises fixed costs for both mines. Since strip mines have a comparative advantage in producing large quantities of coal, the minimum of their average cost curve rises by a smaller amount than the minimum of the average cost curve for shaft mines. The dashed curves in figure 9.1, which reflect the post-legislation situation, show that strip mines can now produce at lower cost than shaft mines. Specifically AC_1' lies everywhere above the minimum of the average cost per AC_0'.

The result of the legislation was to raise costs for all firms, but to raise them relatively more for shaft mines. Since firms care primarily about their costs relative to those of their rivals, legislation was a profit-increasing intervention as far as strip mines were concerned, but a profit-decreasing intervention as far as shaft mines were concerned. Once again, relative comparisons, rather than absolute comparisons, become key in determining the firm's view toward labor intervention.

While the point is quite general and need not be applied to labor cost intervention, the labor angle yields an additional twist. In this situation labor representatives would favor or oppose labor legislation, depending on whether they represented workers in strip mines or shaft mines. Labor unions representing strip mine workers would lobby in favor of legislation, whereas those representing shaft mine workers would lobby against it.

A final example arises when pattern bargaining is used. In the airline industry, unions would often pick one airline and negotiate with it. Other airlines' contracts would then follow the terms set by the first. Thus, if the machinists decide to negotiate with United Airlines, American Airlines wants United to hold firm. But a strike against United means that all of the costs are borne by United. American not only enjoys lower wages as a result of United's tenacity but also gets United's passengers during the period of the strike against United. Until recently airlines, recognizing that pattern bargaining was an attempt by unions to create relative pressures on an airline by leaving its competitors untouched, offset this by making direct transfers to one another. Thus American would share some of its increased revenue with United to strengthen United's resolve. It is the fact that demand shifts easily from one airline to another that allows pattern bargaining to be effective. Again it is the relative comparison that matters.

10   Extensions

This chapter discusses work that has not yet been completed. I will outline some directions for future research and will provide some preliminary analyses. The final part of the chapter will list some topics that I believe should be explored, and I will try to point out some directions in which the research might go.

Multiskilling and Centralization of Authority

Organization scholars have been interested in power in organizations for many years.[1] A specific question relates to the centralization of authority within an organization. When should a firm delegate power to its workers, and when should the firm insist that all decisions be made at the top?

Incentives are important in firms, and I believe that motivational issues are key. But beyond motivation are issues that relate to the organization of work. In this section I focus on one such issue, namely the amount of discretion that a worker should be given over decisions that affect the entire firm. Even if motivation were not a problem, differences in worker ability would provide a rationale for separating decision making from other tasks in the firm. But the separation carries with it some costs. Personnel economics should provide some insight on the trade-off.

Some organizations are more hierarchical than others. One firm may insist that all workers of one type report directly to a worker of another type who has the authority to approve or reverse decisions. Another firm may allow workers to make decisions for themselves, without obtaining higher-level approval. The first organization is often referred to as a top-down organization. The second type of organization is a bottom-up organization. Bottom-up organizations generally do not have low-level workers deciding what high-level workers should do; they merely allow lower-level workers a great deal of discretion in decision making. In fact, if low-level workers decide what high-level workers should be doing, then one can simply redefine which workers are "high" level and which workers are "low" level. Most universities are bottom-up organizations. This is particularly true of research universities, where professors decide the duties, hours, and determine the output of their activities without much direct supervision. Manufacturing plants, on the other hand, tend to be much more hierarchical, where a given worker is told by higher authorities how production should occur. Whether this distinction generalizes to comparisons between manufacturing and services in general remains to be seen. Still it is important to be able to characterize the circumstances under which an organization will give some workers a great deal of discretion over their decisions.[2]

The solution trades off three factors: analytic ability, information, and communication. The employees who make the best decisions may be the ones at the top of the firm. But the persons with the best information may be those at the bottom of the firm, perhaps because they are closer to the customers. The transfer of information from those who gather it to those who can best process it requires communication, which takes time. Indeed the time required to transmit an ungarbled message may be great.

Computer operations provide a metaphor for the problem. Computers are limited by three factors. They are CPU speed, which is analogous to analytic ability; disk size, which is analogous to the information reservoir; and speed of communication which links one part of the computer (e.g., the disk drive) with another part of the computer (e.g., the central processor). In computer networks, slow machines with their own disk drives are often linked to a fast central processor through a communications network. In the absence of resource constraints, it is better to keep all information in RAM of the fastest machine so that the central processor can access it more rapidly. But there are costs involved. Using memory rather than disk for data storage is more expensive.

Similarly communication time can be cut if the top people in the firm also have the relevant information. But this requires that more top-level people gather data. Their comparative advantage is likely to be in decision making rather than in data gathering, so this strategy reduces efficiency. Conversely, the data gatherers could be permitted to make their own decisions in a completely decentralized environment. While saving communication time, and assigning decision making to those who have the information, this approach has the drawback that decisions are made by those with a comparative disadvantage in analysis. This would be like replacing a fast 486 processor with a slower 286 processor to avoid having to communicate with the 486 processor which is housed in another computer.

The delegation of authority is closely connected to the issue of multi-skilling.[3] When multiskilling is pervasive, workers engage in a large number of tasks. Since they are performing many tasks, communication from one worker to another is less important. Take an extreme case where every worker does every task within the firm. Each worker is like his own tiny firm. Communication is likely to be much less important in this organization, and independence is likely to be greater. While this is not a necessary consequence of multiskilling, it is a likely one. There are of course counterexamples. Consider fruit pickers who pick and carry their picked fruit to a central storage area. Each picker is also a carrier, so he need not communicate with carriers to tell them when to pick up the recently picked fruit. But a limited amount of communication may still need to occur. Pickers must decide how to divide up the orchard and must resolve traffic problems when more than one picker arrives at the central storage bin at the same time. Rules may substitute for discretion in many of these circumstances (e.g., in California, when two cars arrive at a stop sign simultaneously, the car to the driver's right has the right of way). Thus, while communication and multiskilling are not the same topic, they are likely to be related and correlated across firms.

A stylized model captures the essence of the problem. Suppose that every firm in the economy is identical and must employ two workers. Output for a work force less than two is zero and output for a work force greater than two is the same as output when exactly two are employed.

Each of the firms has two tasks to be performed, say, thinking and data gathering, and each requires eight hours of labor. The firm may assign one worker to each task, or allow both workers to perform both tasks. Put differently, the firm can use either specialization or multiskilling as technologies.

If multiskilling is used, one unit of output is produced. If, instead, workers are assigned to specific tasks, then output is

$$Q = (1 + \gamma)(1 + t), \qquad \gamma, t > 0. \tag{10.1}$$

The first term, $1 + \gamma$, reflects the gains from specialization. Since $\gamma > 0$, specializing allows output to be higher than it otherwise would be. In the language of the computer metaphor, specialization allows all processing to be done by the high-speed CPU and all data to be stored on the largest disk. The fast computer is not restricted to using only those data that it can keep in memory (RAM), nor is the computer that has the large disk drive required to rely on its own CPU for processing.

In organizations, specialization allows workers to work to their comparative advantages. All thinking can be done by the most efficient thinkers, and all data gathering can be done by the most efficient data gatherers. The disadvantage of specialization is that communication costs t are involved.

In the computer context, it is quicker for the CPU to retrieve information from memory than it is for it to access the disk. While the disk may contain more information, accessing it takes more time. Similarly, in the context of the firm, specialization requires more communication between workers. Each time the data gatherer passes information to the thinker for analysis, the data gatherer must offer details and an explanation. This requires time t, so output is only $1 - t$ times what it would be were no time devoted to communication.

Whether a firm will choose to multiskill and to avoid communication costs by giving much discretion to each worker, or instead to specialize and bear communication costs, depends on the size of γ and t. A firm will choose to specialize and assign thinking to specific workers when the following condition holds:

$$(1 + \gamma)(1 - t) > 1,$$

or equivalently,

$$\gamma - \frac{t}{1 - t} > 0. \tag{10.2}$$

If (10.2) holds, then the gains from using a hierarchical structure where decisions are centralized outweigh the communication costs associated with that structure.

Structuring Integration within an Organization

The relation in (10.2) gives rise to the following proposition:

Proposition 10.1 Hierarchical structures tend to be found in firms where the gains from specialization are large.

Proof The proof follows directly from expression (10.2), which varies directly with γ, the measure of gains from specialization.

In firms where there is a great deal to be gained by assigning thinking to some individuals and data gathering to others, it pays to bear communication costs. Thinkers must communicate to data gatherers not only what needs to be done but the kind of information that the thinkers will need to make decisions. Data gatherers in turn must report their findings to thinkers who then use the information to make decisions. A firm of this sort looks hierarchical.

At the other extreme are firms where all workers do exactly the same thing. In these firms there are no specialized tasks assigned to workers. Each worker does every task, reducing the amount of communication that occurs.

This may suggest that makers of basic goods are likely to be centralized and hierarchical, removing the decision making from those who produce the goods. Consider a large farming operation. The individual who is in the fields working the land has a comparative advantage in raw labor but a large comparative disadvantage in decision making. While the field hands do have better information on current soil and crop conditions, they are so much worse at making decisions that it pays to have a highly centralized structure where decisions are made at the top. Some other results follow as well:

Proposition 10.2 As the costs of communication rise, a decentralized structure becomes more likely.

Proof The proof of the basic proposition is trivial, again following directly from (10.2). Differentiating the left-hand side of (10.2) with respect to t yields

$$\frac{\partial}{\partial t} = -\frac{1}{(1-t)^2},$$

so higher costs make the condition less likely to hold.

Research institutions tend to be highly decentralized, giving a great deal of discretion to the individual researchers. This follows from propositions 10.1 and 10.2. In research, the individual who possesses information is usually the one best suited to analyze it. A dean is likely to have a small or nonexistent comparative advantage in analysis over the researchers in his school. Thus, consistent with proposition 10.1, there is little gain from "vertical specialization" of the sort with which hierarchy is associated. It is unlikely to be efficient for a researcher to outline propositions and then turn them over to the dean for completion and proof. Furthermore the individuals who do the research are also in the best position to judge the kind of work that needs to be done.

"Horizontal" specialization is extremely important in the research context. Individuals in a particular subject area do all the tasks associated with research in that subject area, so they are not vertically specialized. But researchers do not work across areas as a general matter, so they are horizontally specialized. Economists do not write about art history. While some centralization may be appropriate, hiring decisions, teaching materials, and choice of research topics are generally delegated to the researchers themselves. It is simply too costly to communicate this information to a central figure who may be unfamiliar with the field in question.

Specialization and hierarchical authority structures appear to go together in international comparisons. At least in terms of folklore, the Japanese engage in multiskilling, and each job is relatively unspecialized. In the United States workers have more rigidly defined jobs and tend to work at the same task for extended periods of time. Coupled with these observations is the claim that Japanese workers have more discretion over decision making than do their American counterparts. If the folklore is to be believed, Japanese firms are vertically unspecialized and less hierarchical. Americans firms are vertically specialized and more hierarchical.

These claims may or may not be true. If the statements are accurate, then they fit the predictions of the model quite well. But even if they hold, the theory is a partial one at best. It is still necessary to explain why one country chooses to specialize and set up a rigid hierarchy, while another chooses to generalize and give its workers more discretion.[4] To understand this, it is necessary to be able to characterize the production functions themselves and to predict the factors that cause them to vary. Specifically, what factors explain the variation in γ and t across countries? This is an open question, but some corollaries follow from proposition (10.2).

Corollary 10.2a Centralized control and rigid hierarchy are most likely when all employees of the firm have similar experiences on which to draw.

A hierarchical structure is less costly to use when decision makers and data gatherers speak the same language. Thus ex ante homogeneity in background and training of the various workers favors ex post specialization. Centralization of decision making implies communication costs, which are lowest when decision makers readily grasp the message conveyed by those with the data.

Military activities provide the best example of a strictly hierarchical organization where all strategic planning is done at the top. But generals and their subordinates tend to speak the same language because the generals were once in the same positions as their subordinates. Communication between stages is relatively cheap, but coordination is extremely important. Both of these factors point to a highly ordered organization with a great deal of communication. All large decisions are made at the top. A platoon leader rarely decides on his own whether to attempt to take the next hill.

Contrast the military example with that of a general consulting firm. Few decisions are made at the top because there is less need for coordination. Further, the broader is the firm, the less able is the individual with the data to communicate easily with the decision maker. One prediction is that general law firms should have more decentralized structures than those that focus on one area like antitrust or securities litigation.

Corollary 10.2b   Technology-induced reductions in the cost of communication promote specialization and hierarchy.

Specialization and hierarchy have become more prevalent over time. In the agrarian economies of preindustrial Europe, firms (or farms) were smaller, and the owner frequently gathered the data and analyzed them himself. Sharecropping of some form was common, and the farmer, who worked the land and gathered the data, would make almost all decisions for himself. The lord or landowner would extract payments from the farmers but would rarely make strategic decisions for the farmer.

The same is true of early textile manufacturing. Each worker could be viewed almost as self-employed, buying from workers at earlier stages of production and selling to those at later stages of production. Not only a good description of the "putting-out" system, this form of organization also described textile manufacture in the northeastern United States during the earlier part of this century.

The work described here is very preliminary, but it provides the flavor of what may come. There are two conspicuous omissions. First, despite the fact that much of the discussion in previous chapters has focused on incentives, there is little mention of incentives here. But it is clear that the choice of centralization or decentralization may have implications for incentives and worker motivation.[5] Second, the specialization that occurs within the firm was based on the assumption of a homogeneous entering work force. But workers may differ in the characteristics that they bring into the firm. In the university context an individual who was trained in economics cannot teach physics. These specialties are of course affected by the organization of production in firms, since workers can choose their formal training programs. But the fact that workers have become more heterogeneous and specialized over time, even before they enter the firm, may have implications for the organization of the firm.

Product or Function?

Some firms are organized along product lines, whereas others are organized along function lines. For example, consider a large conglomerate like Japan's Mitsubishi. One division produces automobiles, another division produces television sets. It is possible to have some subset of the individuals who work in the automobile division interact with one another, while those who work in television production could interact with one another.

An alternative is to have all of the accountants who do cost accounting form one group, irrespective of whether the accounting is done for the television division or for the automobile division. Particularly in the case of fields like cost accounting, it may make more sense to group by function rather than by product, since accountants may have to take account of both products in order to allocate costs correctly. Organizing on the basis of function ensures that individuals with the right background are involved in all decisions, but these individuals will not have as much information about a particular product as they would were they to focus on one product line.

In some respects the trade-offs seem similar to those involved with specialization and delegation, but they are quite different. The issues here involve not so much whether individuals have control but rather how they exercise their power. Earlier, in discussing industrial politics, I pointed out that cooperation occurs within teams, but not between teams. What is also true is that competition occurs between rivals who are in line for the same job. Thus whether a firm is organized along product lines or function lines has implications for the way in which individuals will interact within the firm.

Once again sports provide a useful analogy. Consider the typical soccer game between two national teams, say, Sweden and Finland. Occasionally arguments and fights occur between the players, but fights are rare between players on the same team. The incentive structure motivates players instead to work well with one another, but to work against their rivals on other teams.

The same is true in an organization. If a team is formed and if compensation is based on the performance of the team, then individuals within that team will tend to cooperate with one another but will be competitive with other teams. Thus it is important to put individuals together when cooperation between them is important.

Families do this quite effectively in the area of the household.[6] Since one member's well-being depends in large part on the total amount of resources available to the nuclear family, individuals tend to be very loyal to other family members. On the other hand, families sometimes feud with one another, and loyalty rarely carries across family lines.

The Structure of Contests within Organizations

Earlier an example was presented in which structuring contests between two players whose abilities differ too greatly resulted in both players reducing their effort. If one player knew that he had little chance of winning, he essentially gave up and accepted the loser's prize. Subsequently the more able player reduced his effort as well, knowing that his opponent was not likely to put up much of a fight.

By choosing opponents appropriately, effort can be affected positively. Thus, if the firm's hierarchical structure is set up appropriately, more output will result. There are at least two ways in which structures can be organized. One is across individuals and the other is over time. Again the sports metaphor is useful.

Consider Swedish soccer. There are a number of teams, all of which vie for the right to play in the finals. Suppose that the league were organized as follows. There are four teams: Djurgården, AIK, GAIS, and Malmö FF. The first two teams are Stockholm teams, the second two teams are non-Stockholm teams. If the league is organized so that the winner from Stockholm plays the winner from outside Stockholm, AIK may give up halfway through the season when it realizes that Djurgården has already secured the top Stockholm spot with virtual certainty. However, if all four teams compete during the first half of the season to play the winner of the team competition from the second half of the season, then AIK may give up for the last couple of weeks of the first half of the season but will play with renewed effort after the second half begins. Whether organizing the league on the basis of geography or dividing it up over time provides better incentives depends on relative variances. When leagues are organized over time, three of the four teams may give up, but for very short periods of time. When leagues are organized across regions, fewer teams give up, but for longer periods of time. A sketch of how the issue is modeled is presented.

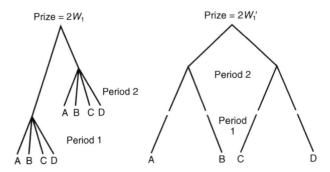

Figure 10.1

Suppose that there are four contestants, A, B, C, D, and two time periods, 1 and 2. There are (at least) two ways to structure the tournament. In game 1 all four contestants compete against one another, and the winner of that round becomes a finalist. The same occurs in period 2, and the winners of rounds 1 and 2 compete for the championship. In each round the cost of effort is $C(\mu)$ and the expected value of being in the finals, which equals one-half of the championship prize, is given by w_1; in other words, the overall winner receives $2w_1$. The prize associated with failing to make the finals is $2w_2$. The situation is shown as game 1 in figure 10.1.

An alternative is to split the contestants into two leagues. One league has A and B, the other has C and D. Competition in each league lasts two periods. The two teams winning their league competition at the end of the two periods compete in the finals, where the winner receives the championship prize, equal to $2w_1'$. Note that $w_1' \neq w_1$ in general, since a different optimal prize structure can be set up for each game. The situation is shown as game 2 in figure 10.1.

The mathematics of game 1 are as follows: Recall that winning the tournament carries with it a prize of $2w_2$, which the winner of each period's game receives with probability $\frac{1}{2}$. Thus in each period each player wants to maximize

$$Pw_1 + (1 - P)w_2 - C(\mu),\tag{10.3}$$

where P is the probability of beating the three other contestants.[7] The first-order condition for A, as before, is

$$(w_1 - w_2)\frac{\partial P}{\partial \mu_A} - C'(\mu_A) = 0. \tag{10.4}$$

Now P is the probability that A beats all three rivals, which is

$$P = \text{Prob}(\mu_A + \varepsilon_A > y_3 + \mu^*)$$

$$= \text{Prob}(\mu_A - \mu^* + \varepsilon_A > y_3) \tag{10.5}$$

$$= \text{Prob}(\varepsilon_A > y_3 - \mu_A + \mu^*),$$

where μ^* is the equilibrium level of effort by rivals and y_3 is the highest order statistic based on independent luck components ε_B, ε_C, and ε_D. The distribution of the third-order statistic is simply $[F(y)]^3$ with density $3[F(y)]^2 f(y)$. Then (10.5) becomes

$$P = \int_{-\infty}^{\infty} \int_{y_3 - \mu_A + \mu^*}^{\infty} 3F(y_3)^2 f(y_3) f(\varepsilon_A)\, d\varepsilon_A\, dy_3$$

$$= 3 \int_{-\infty}^{\infty} F(y_3)^2 f(y_3)[1 - F(y_3 - \mu_a + \mu^*)]\, dy_3.$$

It follows that

$$\frac{\partial P}{\partial \mu_A} = 3 \int_{-\infty}^{\infty} F(y_3)^2 f(y_3) f(y_3 - \mu_a + \mu^*)\, dy_3,$$

which, in equilibrium where $\mu_A = \mu^*$, is simply

$$\frac{\partial P}{\partial \mu_A} = 3 \int_{-\infty}^{\infty} [F(y_3)f(y_3)]^2\, dy_3.$$

The worker then sets effort such that

$$C'(\mu_A) = 3(w_1 - w_2) \int_{-\infty}^{\infty} [F(y_3)f(y_3)]^2\, dy_3. \tag{10.6}$$

Since there is only one w_1 and w_2 for this game, effort is the same in each period and can be set to the first-best level merely by choosing w_1 and w_2 so that

$$3(w_1 - w_2) \int_{-\infty}^{\infty} [F(y_3)f(y_3)]^2\, dy_3 = 1 \tag{10.7a}$$

and

$$(\tfrac{1}{4})(2w_1) + (\tfrac{3}{4})(2w_2) = C(\mu^*). \tag{10.7b}$$

Equation (10.7a) says that since the social value of a unit of output equals 1, $C'(\mu_A) = 1$ must hold at the first best. Equation (10.7a) chooses w_1 and w_2 so as to guarantee it. Equation (10.7b) simply clears the market so that workers are just indifferent between entering and not entering the tournament. Ex ante, each player has a $\frac{1}{4}$ chance of winning and a $\frac{3}{4}$ chance of losing. Winning carries prize $2w_1$, and losing carries prize $2w_2$.

Next look at game 2. This is a 2×2 game, but output is additive over periods. The player's maximization problem is, in period 1,

$$\text{Max}_{\mu_{A_1}} P_1' w_1' + (1 - P_1') w_2' - C(\mu_{A_1}) - C(\mu_{A_2}), \tag{10.8a}$$

and in period 2,

$$\text{Max}_{\mu_{A_2}} P_2' w_1' + (1 - P_2') w_2' - C(\mu_{A_2}), \tag{10.8b}$$

where μ_{A_t} is effort by A in period t and P_t is the probability of winning both rounds as seen in period t. The player in period 1 knows that he will solve (10.8b) in period 2 and so chooses μ_A, taking the solution to (10.8b) into account. In period 2 the player solves

$$\frac{\partial P_2'}{\partial \mu_A}(w_1' - w_2') - C'(\mu_{A_2}) = 0. \tag{10.9a}$$

Given the solution, the player then solves

$$\frac{\partial P_1'}{\partial \mu_{A_1}}(w_1' - w_2') - C'(\mu_{A_1}) = 0, \tag{10.9b}$$

knowing that the choice of μ_{A_1} affects μ_{A_2} through (10.9a).

In period 1 none of the random components is known, so the probability of winning as seen in period 1 is merely

$$P_1(\mu_{A_1} + \mu_{A_2} + \mu_{B_1} - \mu_{B_2} > \xi_1),$$

where ξ_1 is just some random variable with mean zero and

$$\xi_1 = \varepsilon_{B_i} + \varepsilon_{B_2} - \varepsilon_{A_1} - \varepsilon_{A_2}.$$

In period 2 the situation is different. Player A will have observed ε_{A_1} and ε_{B_1} before μ_{A_2} must be chosen. So the relevant probability of winning as seen in period 2 is

$$P_2(\mu_{A_1} + \mu_{A_2} - \mu_{B_1} - \mu_{B_2} + \varepsilon_{A_1} - \varepsilon_{B_1} > \varepsilon_{B_2} - \varepsilon_{A_2}).$$

Define $\xi_2 \equiv \varepsilon_{B_2} - \varepsilon_{A_2}$. The density function of ξ_2 cannot in general be the same as that of ξ_2. Thus

$$\frac{\partial P_1}{\partial \mu_{A_1}} \neq \frac{\partial P_2}{\partial \mu_{A_2}}$$

for $\mu_{A_1} = \mu_{A_2}$ in general. For efficiency, $C'(\mu_{A_1}) = C'(\mu_{A_2}) = 1$, which implies that $\mu_{A_1} = \mu_{A_2}$. But if there is only one prize structure, it is impossible to tailor each period's effort appropriately. Thus both first-order conditions cannot be satisfied simultaneously at $C' = 1$, and the two-league structure is inefficient.

The result is that it is better to divide a tournament into periods where a period is defined as that amount of time necessary to observe a luck component. Once part of the randomness becomes known, individuals reoptimize. When each period is a separate contest, luck becomes truly random and incentives are preserved.

Let us apply this analysis to workers in corporations. Once it becomes clear that one individual has a very high probability of winning the (only) promotion, incentives suffer. After luck is known, any wage spread that provides large enough incentives to put forth efficient effort before luck and other unobservables become known provides the wrong incentives. If, however, promotions are temporary, then workers may compete again when the new round begins. Promotions can be temporary to the extent that jobs are wage slots, rather than task assignments. Winning the promotion simply means that a particular worker receives the largest bonus in a given year. But once January 1st comes around, the slate is wiped clean and workers can compete again.

It is better to use short periods for evaluation and bonuses. Doing so prevents workers from basing their effort on the observed outcome of previous competitions. If previous competition can affect the worker's probability of winning in this time period, then workers who have done well in early rounds will put forth different amounts of effort from those who did poorly. If workers are sorted into contests such that they are ex ante identical (there are incentives reasons to sort them in this way), then in equilibrium workers differ only on the basis of luck. But if this is true, the effort that is optimal for one is also optimal for another. Any bonus competition that induces ex ante identical workers to put forth different amounts of effort cannot be optimal.

The Details of Work Organization

The Selection of Groups of Workers

Sometimes, the activities of firms require that more than one worker must be selected as winner. A number of examples come to mind. Suppose that a university would like to set up a prestigious institute of economics where the members are to be the top economists in the university and the institute can have up to five members. Suppose further that they decide to hold a competition among the fifty existing economists, challenging them to write a paper during the next year. The authors of the best papers are to be awarded positions in the institute. The amount of effort that the economists will put into writing the paper depends on the prize. As such, this resembles a tournament where multiple winners are selected. Suppose further that the number of winners is stochastic. It can be as large as five, but if five good candidates are not found, the institute can be smaller.

A second example is that of a firm that would like to create a supervisory work force from its current pool of one hundred production workers. Suppose that there are no supervisors at the current time and that the firm has a very bottom-heavy structure with only a few managers, the rest of the work force consisting of production workers. The number of supervisors is variable, but management decides to set a maximum of one supervisor per every five workers, meaning that no more than twenty supervisors will be chosen. The firm may set up a contest between the hundred production workers, either implicitly or explicitly.

The tournament model is unwieldy and not well suited to this problem for two reasons. First, tournaments that select, say, five from a group of fifty require analysis of the forty-fifth-order statistic. Each worker competes against what he assumes will be the sixth highest (or 45th from the bottom) player. He does not know nor care about the identity of that player but merely is concerned with that worker's level of output. Order statistics (other than the highest and lowest) have somewhat messy forms and doing comparative statics on them is almost hopeless. Second, since the firm has the option of choosing fewer than five winners, the tournament model, which in this case dictates exactly five winners, is not quite appropriate.

In Lazear (1993) a model is presented to analyze the awards by funding agencies to researchers who apply for grants. Here any number of awards up to A can be given, but the agency need not give away the full complement of A awards. This model is well suited to the selection of a group of workers for prizes. A brief version of that model is presented here.

Think of being awarded one of the positions as being like having one's name drawn in a public lottery. The more tickets that an individual owns, the more likely he is to win one of the positions. Thus let the number of "tickets" that individual i possesses, t_i, be given by

$$t_i = f(\mu_i, \delta_i),\tag{10.10}$$

where μ_i is i's effort and δ_i is i's ability. Both $f_1, f_2 > 0$. The prize associated with winning a position is W, which can be thought of as the present value of the higher wages that go with the promotion.

The total number of tickets T is given by $T = \Sigma t_i$, and the probability that any one worker i will be selected for the promotion is

$$P_i = 1 - \left(1 - \frac{t_i}{T}\right)^A.\tag{10.11}$$

The probability that i's name is called on one particular draw is t_i/T, so $1 - t_i/T$ is the probability that i's name is not called on one draw. Further $(1 - t_i/T)^A$ is the probability of not being called on all A draws, so $1 - (1 - t_i/T)^A$ is the probability of being called at least once. Since a person can hold no more than one position, being called once is as good as being called five times. The expression in (10.11) takes into account that the individual can get no more than one position.[8] While Lazear (1993) considers more general cases, for our purposes it is sufficient to look at the linear situation where $t_i = \mu_i + \delta_i$.

Consider the professors who are hoping to be appointed to the research institute. They want to choose effort μ to maximize their expected net returns:

$$\text{Expected net return} = WP_i - C(\mu),\tag{10.12}$$

where $C(\mu)$ is the cost of effort. Equation (10.12) can be rewritten as

$$\text{Expected net return} = W\left(1 - \left(\frac{1 - t_i}{T}\right)^A\right) - C(\mu)\tag{10.13}$$

with foc,

$$\frac{\partial}{\partial\mu} = W\frac{\partial P_i}{\partial\mu} - C'(\mu) = 0,$$

$$= \frac{WA}{T}\left(1 - \frac{t_i}{T}\right)^{A-1} - C'(\mu) = 0.\tag{10.14}$$

Some results are readily obtained from this formulation. First, let us determine how more able individuals behave as compared with less able individuals. The answer is obtained by looking at $\partial\mu/\partial\delta$ along (10.14). From (10.14) we obtain

$$\frac{\partial\mu}{\partial\delta}\bigg|_{(10.14)} = \frac{-\partial/\partial\delta}{\partial/\partial\mu},$$

or given the current specification,

$$\frac{\partial\mu}{\partial\delta} = -\frac{1}{1 + \{C''T^2/[WA(A-1)(1-(T_i/T))^{A-2}]\}}. \tag{10.15}$$

Since $C'' > 0$, $\partial\mu/\partial\delta$ lies between -1 and 0.

Less able individuals put forth more effort but not enough to eliminate the difference between the more able and less able. More able individuals are more likely to get the position in the institute than less able ones, but their chances do not increase in proportion to their ability. The less able undo some of their disadvantage by working harder on their papers.

Diminishing returns lies at the heart of this result. Even though the cost of effort, as modeled, is no higher to more able individuals, they put forth less of it because the marginal return to effort decreases with t_i. The intuition is clear if we take it to the extreme. Suppose that 5 tickets were to be drawn and that an individual had 99 out of 100 of the outstanding tickets. That person would be almost certain to win one and only one position. There would be virtually no incentive for him to buy additional tickets by putting forth additional effort. The same is not true for the other individual who holds only one of the 100 tickets. He can greatly increase his chances of being appointed by putting forth effort. Since T_i is the sum of effort μ and ability δ, more able people have less to gain from effort.

We can determine quite easily what would happen if the number of positions were increased, while the salary associated with each position were decreased so as to keep expected value the same. The result is that effort by each economist would decline. Even though the expected return is the same, the marginal value of an additional unit of effort declines as the number of positions increases.[9] Again this is a result of diminishing returns. When the number of positions gets very large, every economist is virtually certain to obtain one and only one position. There is no gain to putting forth effort under these circumstances. This means that a structure with a large number of supervisory positions, each of which pays only slightly more than the production worker's wage, will induce less effort than a structure with few supervisory positions, each of which earns a large salary premium.

Many additional results can be obtained by using this model. For example, the effects of giving workers longer planning horizons can be examined. Similarly the effects of giving workers "credit" for good performance on past assignments when doling out current assignments (and pay for them) can also be predicted. These issues are explored in depth in the research context in Lazear (1993).

Internal Promotion versus External Hiring

Many firms give preference to internal candidates for promotion, sometimes promoting an internal person when an outside candidate is superior. Unless differences between candidates are pronounced, insiders usually get the job. Why should a firm favor inside candidates over outside ones? One answer, recently suggested by Chan (1994), is that better incentives are provided to all workers when internal promotions are used over external hiring.

It is easiest to think of this in the context of a tournament. If there is some chance that a worker will be hired into a superior position from the outside, then all workers competing for that job have reduced incentives. The effort decline could be offset by increasing the spread, but risk-averse workers or workers who cannot use capital markets freely prefer smaller rather than larger spreads. As a result it pays to reduce the proportion of individuals who are hired from the outside. This can be shown more formally.

Suppose that workers are risk neutral but that their inability to borrow precludes the firm from using a wage spread between winner and loser that exceeds Z.[10] Suppose further that Z is a binding constraint when all promotion is internal. That is, the solution to the tournament problem yields an optimal wage spread,

$$W_1 - W_2 > Z.$$

Recall that the tournament problem between two workers has worker j maximizing

$$PW_1 - (1 - P)W_2 - C(\mu_j),\tag{10.16}$$

where μ_j is j's effort level. The foc is

$$\frac{\partial P}{\partial \mu_j}(W_1 - W_2) = C'(\mu_j).\tag{10.17}$$

If the probability of internal promotion is π, then

$$P = \pi \operatorname{Prob}[\mu_j - \mu_k > \xi].$$

Now, in symmetric equilibrium, with the constraint binding, the first-order condition becomes

$$\pi g(0) Z = C'(\mu_j), \tag{10.18}$$

where $g(\ )$ is the density of ξ.

Since Z is binding, effort is less than its first-best level, even for $\pi = 1$. Reducing π below one only makes matters worse. Thus allowing for outside hiring, which would reduce the chance that an internal candidate was awarded the superior job, would reduce effort and move the solution away from efficiency.

This analysis implies that firms should favor internal promotion over external hiring. Even if an outsider is better than the internal candidates, a firm is willing to promote the insider in order to improve incentives within the organization. Of course, if the outsider were sufficiently better than the insider, it would pay to sacrifice some (equilibrium) effort and hire the outsider. In general, $\pi < 1$ to accommodate those cases when the outsider has an extremely large advantage over the insider.

There are additional implications as well. A firm's willingness to hire outsiders over insiders depends on the size of the group from which it is promoting. The effect on effort of reducing π below one varies with the number of individuals competing for a particular job. Generally the smaller the number of internal candidates, the larger is the adverse effect on their incentives of hiring from the outside. Offsetting this is that small firms are less likely to have at least one extremely able person among their workers.[11]

Second, the more heterogeneity there is in the population, the more likely is outside hiring. The difference between outsider ability and insider ability must be large and positive in order for the firm to be willing to hire outsiders. Large differences are most likely to be observed when the underlying distribution of ability has fat tails. Thus heterogeneity in the population contributes to outsider hiring and to reduced incentives among insiders.[12]

Worker Participation in Corporate Governance

European countries, Japan, Australia, and New Zealand have had explicit participation by workers in corporate governance for a long period of time. The United States is probably the exception among industrial-ized countries in that it has resisted giving an explicit, mandated role to workers. Still recent changes in the structure of the American corporation have created more flexibility. In this somewhat more open environment workers may obtain an increasing amount of say in what happens in the organization.

There are a number of ways by which workers can exert their influence. Workers may have seats on the boards of directors, allowing workers to affect directly decisions of the firm and perhaps even compensation of the managers. They may have explicit consultation rights through works councils. They may own some of the firm's equity, either directly through ESOPs or indirectly through their pension plans. Personnel practitioners and economists as analysts need a framework in which to think about worker participation.

In some recent work Freeman and Lazear (1994) examine worker partici-pation through the explicit institution of works councils. We attempt to analyze a number of issues. The first question that we address is, If worker participation is valuable, why is it frequently opposed by management? The answer that we provide relies on a trade-off between increasing total rents and affecting distribution of rents between workers and management. While giving workers additional control may increase the total output of the firm, it is difficult to give workers control without also giving them the ability to extract a larger share of the rents. Since management cares not about the total surplus but about the amount of profit that is captured by capital, management may be reluctant to cede power to workers, even if it is socially beneficial to do so. The formal analysis proceeds as follows.

The argument is based on two relations. First, let x denote the amount of power or discretion given to the workers. The rent of the organization R depends on x. If workers are given no discretion, $R = R_0$. With some worker discretion, decisions improve and R rises. If too much worker dis-cretion is given, then rent falls because management does not have enough control over decisions. The result is an $R(x)$ function that has an inverted U-shape, as shown in figure 10.2.

Denote the share of total rent that goes to workers as τ. The share τ also depends on x. It is a standard result of bargaining models (both Nash and Rubenstein)[13] that the share rises with bargaining strength. Thus $\tau(x)$ is monotonically increasing in x. To start, then,

$$R = R(x),$$

$$\tau = \tau(x).$$

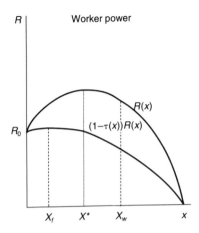

Figure 10.2

Will the firm voluntarily cede the socially optimal amount of power to workers? The answer is no. The firm will give less than x^* power to the council, where x^* is defined as the level of worker power that maximizes joint surplus. Formally, the profit-seeking firm will maximize

$$(1 - \tau(x))R(x),$$

which has the first-order condition

$$-\tau'(x)R(x) + (1 - \tau(x))R'(x) = 0,$$

so

$$R' = \frac{\tau'(x)R(x)}{1 - \tau(x)}. \tag{10.19}$$

Since τ is increasing in x, the right-hand side of (10.19) is positive, which implies that $R' > 0$ at the firm's optimum point. The firm will choose a level of power for the workers on the rising part of the rent-producing curve and voluntarily give workers less power than x^*.[14]

What about workers? If they could choose the amount of power for themselves, would they choose the socially optimal level? Workers who seek to maximize their share of the total surplus $[\tau(x)R(x)]$ will, by symmetry with the analysis of the firm, fail to select the socially optimal point. Workers will choose a level of power that exceeds x^*. They choose x_w in the figure, shortchanging the interests of capital.

Once again industrial politics come into play. Management seeks to give workers too little control over decisions in the firm, but workers would like to have too much power. A third party, such as the government, could impose the optimal solution externally, but this requires a great deal of information on the part of the government itself. Worse, the government does not operate in a vacuum. The outcome of government regulations on worker power is a result of national politics, instead of industrial politics. But national politics, like industrial politics, pit labor against management groups as well, and it is far from clear that the government-imposed solution will be superior to that chosen in the industrial environment.

There are a number of ways by which worker power can increase output of the firm. We focus on three, which are not detailed here. First, by giving workers some say in the way their information is used, workers have better incentives to reveal their preferences truthfully to the firm. This can make both sides better off. Second, firms can communicate information to workers in a more credible way when workers have more authority and better information. Third, the process of discussing issues with workers may result in better solutions because information sets are not completely overlapping. To the extent that workers and management both possess relevant but nonidentical information, formal communication between the parties may increase total output. Once again, while all of these reasons suggest that there are gains from providing power to workers, firms may not choose to do so voluntarily because of the rent loss associated with such a move.

Reductions in Force and Corporate Governance

Many American firms are going through a process of "downsizing," where the work force must be reduced in a relatively short period of time. This can create problems for worker-manager relations. When workers have a voice in corporate governance, the method used for reductions in force (RIFs) can determine whether the policy will succeed or fail.

A reduction in force is most difficult to implement when workers are receiving higher wages at their current firm than they can receive elsewhere. This can come about for one of at least two reasons. First, workers may have specific human capital, where costs and returns to the investment are shared. More senior workers then have wages that exceed their alternatives. Second, if upward-sloping age-earnings profiles are used to

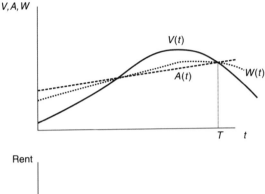

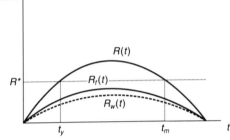

Figure 10.3

generate incentives, then young workers are paid less than they are worth and old workers are paid more than they are worth. An old worker who is laid off receives wages on the new job that are less than the amount he was receiving on the old.

Consider the case of firm-specific human capital. (The case of worker incentives is similar.) Workers are paid less than what they could receive elsewhere initially but more than elsewhere later. This is illustrated in the top panel of figure 10.3.

Workers earn $W(t)$ at the current firm and $A(t)$ at another firm. Consider workers who invest in firm-specific human capital, sharing the costs and benefits with the firm. For expositional convenience, the interest rate is assumed to be zero in the diagram. Wages and alternative wages are given by $W(t)$ and $A(t)$, as defined above. Productivity at the firm is measured by $V(t)$.

In the bottom panel of figure 10.3, we plot the rent as a function of age. Rent should be thought of as the amount of (quasi) rent associated with continuing to work from time t until the retirement date of T. There are two measures of rent. First, since the worker shares in the costs and benefits from the investment in specific human capital, define the worker's rent as

$$R_w(t) = e^{rt} \int_t^T [W(\tau) - A(\tau)]e^{-r\tau} \, d\tau, \tag{10.20}$$

where r is the rate of interest, assumed to be zero in the diagram. The rent that goes to the firm is given by

$$R_f(t) = e^{rt} \int_t^T [V(\tau) - W(\tau)]e^{-r\tau} \, d\tau, \tag{10.21}$$

and total rent is merely the sum of $R_w + R_f = R$, given by

$$R(t) = e^{rt} \int_t^T [V(\tau) - A(\tau)]e^{-r\tau} \, d\tau. \tag{10.22}$$

An efficient layoff rule lays off workers from both ends of the age spectrum. The least total rent is lost by laying off either workers who have not yet invested very much or who are close to retirement. The amount of rent that must be lost depends on the age distribution of the work force and on the size of the RIF. Suppose that efficient layoffs require that every worker who produces less than R^* of (total) rent should be laid off. Then all those who are younger than t_y and older than t_m will lose their jobs if an efficient layoff policy is implemented.

Rather than following a strict reverse seniority layoff pattern, it is efficient to lay off very young and very old workers first. The very young present little problem because they do not possess seniority, but the very old might insist on using their seniority to block their layoffs. There are two ways around this problem. The first is to couple the layoff of older workers with severance pay of the form discussed in chapter 4. The second is to provide workers with some incentive to take capital's interests into account. One way to do this is to make them shareholders.

Suppose that labor owns ρ of the firm, with $1 - \rho$ being held by non-labor interests. Layoffs help labor by increasing the value of the firm, and thereby raising the value of the stock held by labor. But layoffs potentially hurt labor by forcing workers to take another job, the value of which may be lower than the current wage.

Will workers as shareholders vote for an efficient layoff policy? The answer depends on worker age and on stock ownership. All workers whose ages are between t_y and t_m favor the layoffs. They lose nothing by an efficient layoff policy because they are not laid off and gain through the appreciation of their stock.[15] But young workers and old workers who are certain to be laid off may oppose the efficient layoff policy. This depends on the rent lost and on the amount of stock they own. Specifically a worker who is to be laid off votes for the layoff iff

$$R_w(t) < \frac{\rho \Delta K}{L^*},$$ (10.23)

where ΔK is the change in the capital value of the firm associated with implementing the efficient layoff policy and L^* is the number of workers in the firm before the RIF who own stock in the firm.[16]

The right-hand side of expression (10.23) is the worker's capital gain from an efficient layoff policy. There are L^* workers, each of whom is assumed to have an equal stake in the firm. Since ρ is the proportion of the firm owned by labor, the rhs is each worker's individual capital gain.

A worker who is subject to layoff will vote for an efficient layoff policy if his losses in rent associated with the layoff are small relative to his capital gain on the stock he owns. There are a number of implications of this analysis (see Freeman and Lazear 1995), but I focus on one point here: The larger the ownership stake that labor has, the more likely are workers to vote for the layoff.[17] For any given layoff policy, the larger is the right-hand side of (10.23), the more likely is a worker to focus on capital gains rather than on rent lost through unemployment.

If $\rho = 0$ so that workers have no ownership, they do not favor efficient layoffs, but they cannot vote. If $\rho = 1$ so that workers own the entire firm, then workers not targeted for layoff vote for efficient layoff, and those who will be laid off are most likely (as compared with any other ρ) to vote for layoff. But if $\rho = 1$, then the firm goes as labor decides. Shareholders without any labor interest would always prefer the efficient layoff policy: As labor's share in ownership approaches one, the number of votes for an efficient layoff policy declines.

Intermediate cases are more complicated. Without going through the analysis here, it can be shown[18] that it is possible to increase the number of votes for an efficient layoff policy by increasing labor's ownership stake. By increasing labor's share, a large enough proportion of workers may change their votes from no to yes to more than cover the increase in votes given to labor. When a worker switches from a no vote to a yes vote, he votes all of his shares as yes. Furthermore a large group of workers who were on the margin may switch their votes to yes when their stake goes up by just a small amount.

The point is that providing workers with ownership in the firm may actually reduce the industrial relations problems that management has with labor. Giving workers more power provides them with more ability to be obstructionist, if they so desire. But giving them a larger stake in the firm reduces their incentives to be obstructionist. The latter point is especially relevant if worker ownership is tailored to worker age and experience characteristics and if ownership is coupled with the appropriate severance pay policies.

Some Additional Areas for Investigation

In this last section I merely outline some questions that I believe to be fertile ground for future research in personnel economics.

1. Empirical Analysis of Decision Making

There are many decisions that human resource managers must make. How do they make these decisions? Specifically, which factors are most important in determining the way a manager decides whom to hire, whom to fire, and whom to promote? What explains whether firms use formal seniority systems or some other algorithm for assigning people to jobs? Which characteristics are most important in the hiring decision?

2. Task Assignment and Job Design

How are tasks allocated within an organization? Who is assigned responsibility for a particular project? Is the decision based on ability, on the best ideas for that particular project, or on the best set of skills? Does past performance count? If so, how is it rewarded?

Related, how are tasks divided up within the firm? When are workers assigned large, long-term projects rather than small, short-term tasks? Who should be given the role of supervision and evaluation? When does peer evaluation dominate evaluation by supervisors? How much weight should be placed on each group's opinion? How should evaluators be compensated to facilitate objective decision making?

3. Jobs or Individuals

Are individuals hired for specific jobs, or are jobs created for a given individual? How are job descriptions determined, and are they meaningful?

Are job descriptions altered to fit an incumbent? How frequently does this occur? What is the significance for compensation when jobs are reclassified?

4. Creation of Jobs within the Firm

How and when are new positions created within a firm? Is most job growth a result of expansion of existing departments, or does it occur as firms branch out into new areas of business? Conversely, what accounts for contraction in most organizations? Does employment reduction result from neutral cuts across the board, or do most employment decreases come about as firms eliminate one or another division?

5. Hierarchies and Change

Are some hierarchical structures better for some circumstances than others? For example, in industries that are undergoing rapid technological change, one hierarchical structure may be better. Some structures may be rigid and unadaptable but very useful for the exact climate in which they operate. Other structures may be less well suited to a particular business environment but may be much more adaptable. Do we observe different kinds of organizational structures as we look across industries?

6. Life Cycle of the Firm's Occupational Structure

Does the occupational distribution of a firm have a life cycle? One possibility is that the choice of personnel type changes with the age of the firm. When firms are new, they may be dominated by engineers and individuals who focus on research and development. As a firm grows, marketing becomes relatively more important, and the firm hires a larger proportion of sales and advertising experts. Finally, when a firm is mature, financial transactions become relatively more important, and general management and finance may dominate. As an empirical matter, is there a predictable occupational cycle to a firm, and is there a theoretical framework that can explain this pattern?

7. International Differences in Labor Usage

Do industries and/or countries differ in their ability to use particular types of labor? Are some economies better suited to one skill distribution, while other economies are better suited to another skill distribution? For example, the United States has larger variance in its skill mix than does Japan. Folklore has it that the United States is quite strong among highly skilled workers but relatively weak among unskilled workers. Japan, on the other hand, seems to be more homogeneous, having a better bottom end but not quite the number of high-quality individuals at the upper end. Europe may fit somewhere in the middle.

One hardly believes that this is a historical accident. After all, the skill distribution is endogenous. But some population characteristics may be slow to change. Causality is always difficult to establish, but it is important to determine whether industrial structure is determined by the characteristics of the underlying labor force or whether the labor force is a source of flexibility that responds to an exogenously determined industrial structure.

8. Ports of Entry and Mobility within the Firm

Already mentioned in an earlier chapter are "ports of entry" within the firm. Do most individuals get hired in at one level, or are the options for employment open throughout the entire hierarchy? Also, are there specific job paths to the top? Are these based on skills or ability, or do they depend in large part on historical accidents? Is the distinction between line and staff folklore or fact? Is it true that individuals who are classified as staff are less likely to move up the corporate ladder than those individuals who are in line positions?

9. Downward Mobility

Is downward mobility as uncommon in most organizations as conventional wisdom would have it? Under which circumstances are wages lowered? When are individuals demoted? Are titles adjusted, or are wages merely reduced? What is the pattern of "bumping" in organizations? How does it differ by industry, and which factors can be called upon to explain these patterns?

10. Speed of Promotions

How long does it take an individual to move from an entry level job to the highest position that he attains in the firm? How does this vary across organizations?[19] For example, in academics the highest-quality departments seem to promote individuals much more rapidly than the lower-quality departments. Is this a fact and, if so, why? What does it indicate about incentives and performance?

What happens to individuals who are at their highest achieved positions? Do they stagnate and, if so, is multiskilling a potential solution to this problem?

11. Multinational Personnel Issues

Is managing of foreign workers different from managing the native population? How important are cultural factors in determining the ways in which work is organized? If cultural factors are important, which observable variables explain these cultural factors? Are there theoretical models that can rationalize the behavior?

11   Conclusion

These chapters are a sampler of issues that make up traditional questions in personnel but that have been analyzed by economists in recent years. Personnel economics has made rigorous the analysis of many issues that are of general interest, both to economists and to industrial psychologists. But the approaches are very different. Economists look to generalize and to quantify; we abstract from the messy issues and focus on those points that we believe to be key to the problem. Industrial psychologists tend to be more descriptive and encompassing, but the analysis sometimes leaves the reader confused.

The first chapter discusses some philosophical questions. Since personnel economics is in large part normative, developed for use by business-persons, it might appear that its value as a positive analysis is somewhat weakened. I believe—and provide an example to show—that personnel economics can be a very good description of what is, but can also be used to determine what should be. Personnel economists need not be embarrassed by the fact that their theories may have some practical use. The field is a science, and in my view, a good description of what currently occurs in firms.

The substantive part of the book begins with a concentration on compensation issues because much of the early work in personnel economics is on compensation. It is not surprising that compensation is the area that draws the most immediate attention from economists, since we are taught to think in terms of prices and income. Chapter 2 examines fixed versus variable pay. When should pay be tied to input and when to output? What are the appropriate formulas for variable pay, and how do these formulas relate to such factors as risk aversion, capital–labor ratios, and monitoring costs?

In chapter 3 tournament models are introduced. They form the basis of much of the discussion in personnel economics. Their key feature is that compensation is based on relative rather than absolute comparisons. But they are also important in that they lay the groundwork for a rigorous theory based on jobs rather than the individuals who occupy them.

An extension of tournament theory takes us to industrial politics. Since workers care not only about how well they do but also about how well their fellow employees do, tournament-based motivation creates an environment where interaction between workers is important. Sometimes this interaction is negative, and management must understand these interactions in order to tailor their policies to them.

Chapter 4 discusses work life incentive schemes. Compensation can be varied over the work life to induce workers to put forth desired levels of effort. By paying workers less than they are worth when young and more than they are worth when old, workers are motivated to exert effort throughout their entire lifetimes.

Chapter 5 considers teams and team-based compensation. Peer pressure and the payment rule can affect how workers behave in a team setting. Stock options and profit sharing, which are forms of team compensation, can be analyzed. Because free-rider effects are so important in this context, team compensation as a motivator must be structured in a particular way in order to generate any incentives at all. Specific stock option formulas are analyzed with a focus on their incentive effects, both in terms of effort and in terms of their effects on generating risk-taking behavior.

Chapter 6 examines other compensation issues. How much of compensation should be pecuniary, and how much should take other forms? How do workers value fringe benefits, and how does this relate to the firm's costs? What can be learned from commonly used job evaluation indexes that set wages on the basis of job and worker characteristics? How do legal interdictions, such as comparable worth, relate to the indexes?

Beyond these issues, other questions arise. When should bonuses be given, and when should penalties be threatened? Formally, bonuses and penalties appear identical, but I argue that there is a distinction between the two. Furthermore the distinction leads to testable implications and predictions about how firms do or should behave. Finally, this chapter considers some macroeconomic implications of personnel economics, especially as it relates to models with unemployment equilibria.

In chapter 7 the notion of the "job" is introduced. While most businesspersons think that jobs are an important unit of analysis, jobs have been mostly neglected as a subject in theoretical and empirical economics. I hope to change that and present some reasons why it is now time to think in terms of jobs (as well as workers). Different questions arise that require different kinds of data, but much can be learned by thinking about labor markets in this somewhat different way. Human capital theory has dominated labor market theory and empirics for the past thirty years with good reason: It is a parsimonious structure with many implications that have been borne out empirically. Chapter 7 tries to examine some analogous models and empirical predictions that are based on jobs rather than the individuals who occupy them. Questions about intrafirm mobility and wage determination are at the heart of this subject.

Chapter 8 considers job evaluation and performance appraisal. Most workers are evaluated on some regular basis. How frequently are evaluations done, what is the nature of the evaluation, and how do evaluations vary with the underlying characteristics of the workers and the firms?

In chapter 9 labor market institutions are examined. I define labor market institutions to be those forces that operate in the labor market other than through the price system. Tenure, up-or-out rules, and legal constraints are some of the institutions discussed. In the legal context the emphasis is on relative rather than absolute comparisons. A firm or group of workers may favor legislation, not because it makes them so much better off but because it makes their rivals so much worse off. Such is the case with minimum wage legislation and health and safety requirements.

Chapter 10 is speculative. It introduces a number of subjects that have not yet been fully examined. These include a number of new topics, some of which are about the firm's hierarchy and the delegation of authority within organizations, corporate governance and worker participation in it, and internal rather than external promotion. The chapter concludes by listing a number of topics that I believe are important and largely unexplored.

I stated in the introduction that I would emphasize four themes. I repeat those here:

First, personnel economics is in large part normative, but it remains systematic. Since the analysis is appropriate for applied business situations, it can be taught as a prescriptive science as well as a descriptive one. The example presented in chapter 1 illustrates the validity of this point.

Second, a personnel system is an entire structure that can be understood within the economic framework. Since it is an entire structure, it makes no sense to analyze one part without considering other parts. As shown, one cannot discuss the compensation associated with a position without a way to convert nonpecuniary attributes into pecuniary ones. Further, compensation and general treatment of one worker depend on how that worker's worth relates to that of other workers in the firm.

Third, much of the essence of personnel economics depends on relative comparisons rather than on absolute ones. Individuals are compared to one another rather than to some absolute standard. Similarly firms are compared to one another and are not judged on the basis of some absolute criterion. Most of the work on tournaments and industrial politics rests heavily on this theme. The analysis of industrial politics is an outgrowth of this line of reasoning.

Finally, economics is well suited to the study of micro-level human relations. While psychology and sociology may be able to offer insight into much of individual behavior at work, these fields have nothing over economics in their ability to understand human issues that are difficult to quantify. On the contrary, economics can reveal that seemingly straightforward and intuitive explanations of work-related phenomena are often misleading and frequently wrong. There is no reason to cede control over this area of social science to other fields merely because they involve human emotion. Indeed, in writing this book, I hope to convince the reader that personnel economists have much to teach not only other scholars but practitioners as well.

Notes

Chapter 1

1. See Armstrong and Lorentzen (1982).

2. There is now an enormous literature, spawned by some very early papers. Among the earliest are D. G. Johnson (1950), Steven Cheung (1969), and Steven Ross (1973).

3. See Armstrong and Lorentzen (1982), p. 4.

4. In addition to the tournament literature discussed below, see Salop and Sheffrin (1983) for a discussion of the point in the product market context.

5. An important exception is the early work by Gary Becker (1962) and Jacob Mincer (1962) on human capital. While not devoted to the form of compensation, these analyses concentrated on life-cycle patterns of wages, both at the theoretical and empirical levels.

6. See Becker (1975) and Mincer (1974) for a sample of the human capital literature.

7. A rough calculation suggests that this sum would employ about 2000 economists and the complementary capital.

Chapter 2

1. The earliest version of these arguments appeared in Lazear (1986b). More recent papers in the same vein are by Robert Gibbons (1987), Eugene Fama (1991), and Charles Brown (1990, 1992).

2. However, there is a sense in which a reinterpretation of the mathematics in (2.1)–(2.7) yields the sorting result.

3. The fact that a and a' are negative is inconsequential.

4. Fogel and Engerman (1989) apply the same logic to explain the treatment of slaves.

5. While it is often fashionable to assume that workers know their ability levels better than buyers of their labor, I see no obvious justification for this assumption. In fact the reverse argument can be made. Firms see many workers at various stages of their careers; a worker does not have such a large body of data. Firms may be more objective about a worker's ability than the worker himself. The implications for pay schemes are somewhat different

when asymmetric information is assumed. These implications are detailed in Lazear (1986b) and bear a resemblance to Spence's signaling results (1973), where too much measurement is done.

6. Differentiate the left-hand side of (2.9) with respect to w:

$$F(w) + wf(w) - wf(w) = F(w) > 0.$$

7. Ickes and Samuelson (1987) argue that a solution to the ratchet effect is inducing workers to change jobs each period. While this is a solution, it in some sense throws the baby out with the bath water. The whole problem arises when there is some match-specific capital, so workers cannot change jobs costlessly. Inducing separations eliminates the advantages of that match-specific capital and reduces the firm's ability to behave opportunistically.

Chapter 3

1. Tournament theory was introduced by Lazear and Rosen (1981). Nalebuff and Stiglitz (1983) and Green and Stokey (1983) elaborate and examine some implications of the theory.

2. While most of the discussion has been in terms of effort, the term "labor supply" is perfectly appropriate. There is nothing in the mathematics that distinguishes effort per hour from hours per day, days per week, or weeks worked per year. In fact every agency problem is simply a labor supply problem and can be thought of as such. This is true whether the mechanism used to elicit effort is a tournament, a straight piece rate, or some other device. That labor supply is central, while obvious at some level, has been neglected by many authors. It is, in part, responsible for the confusion in the efficiency wage literature, to which I will return later.

3. Milgrom (1988) argues that workers exert effort to influence the decisions made by superiors. Pay compression reduces the incentive to engage in influence activity. Milgrom's theory is not one of worker interaction, since his argument would hold even in an environment where the firm has only one worker whose output must be evaluated. In some related work Prendergast (1992) looks at the incentives for individuals to provide correct evaluations in an organization. He argues that "yes men" may result when evaluators calculate the effect their statements may have on their own positions. In many respects the points here are related to those made by Carmichael (1988), who discusses the value of tenure (see below).

Chapter 4

1. In a sense this is a bogus issue. Promotion slots can always be created to provide incentives for workers throughout their careers. This is just a question of how finely job titles are defined. The discussion of job design will reveal that firms may not be completely free to set up additional job slots.

Chapter 5

1. To the extent that many of the interactions are repeated ones, reputation effects may solve some problems of the short-run opportunistic behavior in team settings.

2. See Bulow and Scholes (1983) for a discussion of pensions using the idea that workers are equity holders within the firm.

3. The technical discussion of this is laid out in Jackson and Lazear (1991).

4. At the extreme the expected value of straight stock that pays off v is equal to zero. An option with strike price K is always worth more than zero because the option can be discarded when $v < K$.

Chapter 6

1. See Fischel and Lazear (1986) for a detailed discussion of comparable worth.

2. Aron and Olivella (1994) have constructed a theory based on the idea that expectations are connoted by language choice.

3. For example, see the work by Raff and Summers (1987) on Henry Ford's experiments with Ford Motor Company.

4. See Bulow and Summers (1986) and also MacLeod and Malcomson (1993).

5. See Akerlof and Katz (1989) for a discussion of bonding and its implications. Bonding need not be observed, since it is only a threat that in equilibrium is not carried out. Whether the threat is made is an empirical question that is difficult to resolve, since threats that are never carried out are difficult to observe.

6. See Lindbeck and Snower (1986).

7. The analysis comes from Lazear (1986a).

8. See Lazear (1986a) for the full exposition.

9. See Greenwald (1986) for a model where lemons are the workers who turn over. What makes Greenwald's model work is that workers can be unemployed either because they are bad workers or because they are good but did not like the work environment of their prior firm.

10. See Lazear (1986a), p. 160.

Chapter 7

1. Much of the empirical material is drawn from Lazear (1992).

2. Kevin J. Murphy (1984) in his Ph.D. dissertation found that jobs are often created to accommodate former CEOs when a new person steps into the CEO position.

3. See Doeringer and Piore (1971), Thurow (1972), and Reder (1955) for an institutional discussion of internal labor markets and job ladders.

4. It is of course possible to base within-job raises on relative comparisons as well. Even within a job category, worker performance can differ and individuals can be, and perhaps are, given raises on the basis of their relative positions.

5. A remaining, unsolved problem appears on the firm side. While Rosen (1986) solves for the worker's behavior, he does so assuming that the firm attempts to elicit the same level of effort at each stage of the contest. But, since effort at higher levels has a higher marginal

product than effort in lower-level jobs, optimal effort probably increases as workers get promoted. Still this is likely to reinforce Rosen's result. If more effort is desired at the top, then the salary distribution would be even more skewed.

6. See Mayer (1960), Miller (1982), and Rosen (1982).

7. This literature was started by Gordon (1974), Azariadis (1975), and Baily (1974).

8. See Thaler and Rosen (1976).

9. See Rosen (1972) for a model that fits this story nicely.

10. See Sattinger (1980).

11. See Milgrom and Roberts (1992) and related Holmstrom and Milgrom (1991).

12. The data are proprietary and the firm's name cannot be released. These results are contained in Lazear (1992).

13. See Mincer and Jovanovic (1981), Gronau (1988), and Hall (1982).

14. See, for example, Topel and Ward (1992).

15. Social output is relevant because competition forces the firm to consider (implicitly) the worker's alternative use of time.

Chapter 8

1. See Armstrong and Lorentzen (1982), p. 266.

2. In *American Nurses Association v. State of Illinois* (1984) a study was conducted in which different groups of evaluators ranked a number of jobs in the hospital environment. The females on the evaluation committee consistently ranked female dominated jobs as being worth more than males did.

3. The major early empirical work on this topic was done by Ferster and Skinner (1957).

4. This discussion is based on Lazear (1990a).

5. This is related to order effects that are of concern to psychologists. See, for example Einhorn and Hogarth (1985).

6. Productive workers who receive a scrambled evaluation earn only one-half over their lifetimes of the amount that they would earn were the evaluation to be accurate.

7. See Lazear (1990b) for a complete analysis of the creditor problem.

Chapter 9

1. See Lazear (1989) and also Abraham and Houseman (1993).

2. In fact in Lazear (1989) I find that the effects are negative and that going to a French style severance pay system would reduce employment in the United States by about three million workers.

3. See Harris and Weiss (1984).

4. See also Kahn and Huberman (1988).

5. The "somewhat" depends on the definition of tenure. If tenure protects the entire wage path so that an individual's compensation within the firm is totally independent of the new hiring decision, then the story holds because tenure eliminates all incentives to hire strategically. Of course, if this were the case, it would be hard to understand how compensation could be relative in any sense within the firm. So tenure is likely to be only a partial cure for this problem.

6. Siow (1993) argues that in universities, tenure is one of a number of institutions that deal with informational asymmetries that arise because of the nature of research and teaching.

7. See Hall and Lazear (1984) for an early discussion of the problem.

8. This structure is presented in Hall and Lazear (1984).

9. See Salop and Sheffrin (1983).

10. See Neumann and Nelson (1982) for a discussion of this legislation.

Chapter 10

1. See Pfeffer (1992) and Rotemberg (1993).

2. See Aoki (1986) for an early discussion of these issues.

3. See Carmichael and MacLeod (1989) for a discussion of the issue.

4. The phenomenon is especially puzzling, since in almost all other respects Japanese society is much more formal and hierarchical than American society. Even in the industrial context hierarchy seems to be more important in Japanese organizations. Senior members of the firm speak before junior members do. In American organizations the rules seem to be less rigid. Even the Japanese language has a structure that implies hierarchy. So either the facts are wrong, or one must explain why one part of society is hierarchical and the other is not.

5. Itoh (1992) focuses almost exclusively on incentives and downplays comparative advantage in his model of delegation of authority.

6. See Becker (1991).

7. We ignore the probability of winning twice, which for large numbers of contestants is trivial.

8. It is based on sampling with replacement. As long as the number of players is large, this assumption is appropriate.

9. See Freeman and Lazear (1995).

10. Recall that for sufficiently large wage spreads, the worker is required to "ante." His ante and that of his rival are paid to him if he wins. But paying an ante may require borrowing.

11. The value of the highest-order statistic of ε_i is monotonically increasing in the number of draws.

12. This follows because the highest-order statistic increases with mean-preserving spreads in the underlying distributions.

13. We are grateful to Peter Cramton for pointing this out.

14. The reader will notice that this contradicts the Coase theorem (1960) in which two parties to an arrangement are expected to maximize the joint surplus through some means or other. By giving the two sides only one tool to produce the joint surplus and divide it, we have ruled out such an arrangement.

15. It is assumed that the layoff is a once-and-for-all policy. Otherwise, workers who are close to the layoff cutoff ages might fear that they will be the first ones let go in subsequent layoffs, inducing them to vote against this layoff.

16. For simplicity, each worker is assumed to have the same proportion of stock. This assumption can be altered. Indeed, if workers had different amounts of shares, efficient voting behavior could be induced by all workers.

17. This does not imply that the larger the worker ownership, the more likely are desirable layoffs to occur. There are two effects: A worker is never more likely to vote for an efficient layoff than a nonlabor owner of capital. But giving workers more ownership makes each worker more inclined to vote for layoffs. This is detailed below.

18. Again see Freeman and Lazear (1995).

19. See McCue (1994), who analyzes wage growth and promotion.

References

Abraham, Katharine, and Susan N. Houseman. 1993. Does employment protection inhibit labor market flexibility? Lessons from Germany, France, and Belgium. NBER Working Paper 4390. June.

Akerlof, George A., and Lawrence F. Katz. 1989. Workers' trust funds and the logic of wage profiles. *Quarterly Journal of Economics* 104(3):525–36.

American Nurses Association, et al. v. State of Illinois, et al. 1984. 84 C 4451 in the United States District Court for the Northern District of Illinois, Eastern Division. Affidavit of Edward P. Lazear, July 30.

Aoki, Masahiko. 1986. Horizontal versus vertical information structure of the firm. *American Economic Review* 76(5):971–83.

Armstrong, Michael, and John F. Lorentzen. 1982. *Handbook of Personnel Management Practice.* Englewood Cliffs, NJ: Prentice-Hall.

Aron, Debra, and Pau Olivella. 1994. Bonus and penalty schemes as equilibrium incentive devices, With application to manufacturing systems. *Journal of Law, Economics, and Organization,* 10, Spring:1–34.

Asch, Beth. 1990. Do incentives matter? The case of navy recruiters. *Industrial and Labor Relations Review* 43 (special issue):89–106.

Athey, Susan, Joshua Gans, Scott Schaefer, and Scott Stern. 1994. The allocation of decisions in organizations. Stanford University. Stanford University Graduate School of Business Research Paper 1322. October.

Azariadis, Costas. 1975. Implicit contracts and underemployment equilibria. *Journal of Political Economy* 83:1183–1202.

Baily, Martin Neil. 1974. Wages and employment under uncertain demand. *Review of Economic Studies* 41:37–50.

Baker, George, Michael Gibbs, and Bengt Holmstrom. 1994b. The wage policy of a firm. *Quarterly Journal of Economics* 109:921–55.

Baker, George, Michael Gibbs, and Bengt Holmstrom. 1993. Hierarchies and compensation: A case study. *European Economic Review* 37:366–78.

Baker, George, Michael Gibbs, and Bengt Holmstrom. 1994a. The internal economics of the firm: Evidence from personnel data. *Quarterly Journal of Economics* 109:881–919.

Baker, George. 1992. Incentive contracts and performance measurement. *Journal of Political Economy* 100:598−614.

Becker, Gary S. 1991. *A Treatise on the Family*, enl. ed. Cambridge: Harvard University Press.

Becker, Gary S. 1975. *Human Capital: A Theoretical and Empirical Analysis, with Special Reference to Education*, 2d ed. New York: Columbia University Press for National Bureau of Economic Research.

Becker, Gary S. 1962. Investment in human capital: A theoretical analysis. *Journal of Political Economy* 70:9−49.

Benelli, Giuseppe, Claudio Loderer, and Thomas Lys. 1987. Labor participation in corporate policy-making decisions: West Germany's experience with codetermination. *Journal of Business* 60:553−75.

Bergson, Abram. 1978. Managerial risks and rewards in public enterprises. *Journal of Comparative Economics* 2:211−25.

Blau, Francine D. 1984. Occupational segregation and labor market discrimination: A critical review. In Barbara Reskin, ed., *Sex Segregation in the Workplace: Trends, Explanations, Remedies*. Washington: National Academy Press, pp. 117−43.

Brown, Charles. 1990. Firms' choice of method of pay. *Industrial and Labor Relations Review* 43:165S−82S.

Brown, Charles. 1992. Wage levels and methods of pay. *Rand Journal* 23:366−75.

Bull, Clive, Andrew Schotter, and Keith Weigelt. 1987. Tournaments and piece rates: An experimental study. *Journal of Political Economy* 95:1−33.

Bulow, Jeremy, and Myron Scholes. 1983. Who owns the assets in a defined-benefit pension plan? In Zvi Bodie and John Shoven, eds., *Financial Aspects of the U.S. Pension System*. Chicago: University of Chicago Press for NBER, pp. 17−36.

Bulow, Jeremy I., and Lawrence H. Summers. 1986. A theory of dual labor markets with application to industrial policy, discrimination, and keynesian unemployment. *Journal of Labor Economics* 4:376−414.

Carmichael, H. Lorne. 1989. Self-enforcing contracts, shirking and life cycle incentives. *Journal of Economic Perspectives* 3:65−83.

Carmichael, H. Lorne. 1988. Incentives in academics: Why is there tenure? *Journal of Political Economy* 96:453−72.

Carmichael, H. Lorne 1981. Implicit contracting and seniority rules. Ph.D. dissertation. Stanford University.

Carmichael, H. Lorne. 1983. Firm-specific human capital and promotion ladders. *Bell Journal* 14:251−58.

Carmichael, H. Lorne, and Bentley W. MacLeod. 1989. Multiskilling, technical change, and the Japanese firm. Queen's University. December.

Chan, William. 1994. External recruitment vs. internal promotion. Hong Kong University. *Journal of Labor Economics*, forthcoming.

Cheung, Steven N. S. 1969. *The Theory of Share Tenancy: With Special Application to Asian Agriculture and the First Phase of Taiwan Land Reform*. Chicago: University of Chicago Press.

Coase, Ronald H. 1960. The problem of social cost. *Journal of Law and Economics* (October):1–44.

Doeringer, P., and M. Piore. 1971. *Internal Labor Markets and Manpower Analysis*. Lexington, MA: D.C. Heath.

Ehrenberg, Ronald G., and Michael L. Bognanno. 1990. Do tournaments have incentive effects? *Journal of Political Economy* 98(6):1307–24.

Einhorn, Hillel, and Robin Hogarth. 1985. A contrast-surprise model for updating beliefs. Working Paper. Graduate School of Business, University of Chicago. April.

Elton, Jeffrey J. 1991. Retail broker compensation with firm marketing investment: Adjusting earnings and payout percentages for firm capital contributions to broker production. Ph.D. dissertation. University of Chicago.

Fama, Eugene F. 1980. Agency problems and the theory of the firm. *Journal of Political Economy* 88:288–307.

Fama, Eugene F. 1991. Time, salary, and incentive payoffs in labor contracts. *Journal of Labor Economics* 9:25–44.

Farrell, Joseph, and Suzanne Scotchmer. 1988. Partnerships. *Quarterly Journal of Economics* 103:279–97.

Ferster, Charles B., and B. F. Skinner. 1957. *Schedules of Reinforcement*. New York: Appleton-Century-Crofts.

Fischel, Daniel, and Edward P. Lazear. 1986. Comparable worth and discrimination in the labor market. *Chicago Law Review* 53:891–918.

Fogel, Robert William, and Stanley L. Engerman. 1989. *Time on the Cross: The Economics of American Negro Slavery*. New York: Norton.

Freeman, Richard B., and Edward P. Lazear. 1995. Relational investing: The worker's perspective. In Ronald Gilson, John C. Coffee and Louis Lowenstein, eds., *Meaningful Relationships: Institutional Investors, Relational Investing and the Future of Corporate Governance?* New York: Oxford University Press, forthcoming.

Freeman, Richard B., and Edward P. Lazear. 1994. An Economic Analysis of Works Councils. In Joel Rogers and Wolfgang Streeck, eds., *Works Councils: Consultation, Representation, and Cooperation in Industrial Relations*. Chicago: University of Chicago Press for NBER. forthcoming 1995.

Friedman, Milton. 1953. *Essays in Positive Economics*. Chicago: University of Chicago Press.

Gaynor, Martin, and Mark V. Pauly. 1990. Compensation and productive efficiency in partnerships: Evidence from medical group practice. *Journal of Political Economy* 98(3):544–73.

Gibbons, Robert. 1987. Piece-rate incentive schemes. *Journal of Labor Economics* 5(4)1:413–29.

Gibbons, Robert, and Lawrence F. Katz. 1991. Layoffs and lemons. *Journal of Labor Economics* 9:351–80.

Gibbons, Robert and Kevin J. Murphy. 1990. Relative performance evaluation for chief executive officers. *Industrial and Labor Relations Review* 43(special issue):30s–51s.

Gibbs, Michael John. 1989. Promotions, compensation and firm organization. Ph.D. dissertation. University of Chicago.

Gilson, Ronald J., and Robert H. Mnookin. 1985. Sharing among the human capitalists: An economic inquiry into the corporate law firm and how partners split profits. *Stanford Law Review* 37:313–92.

Goldin, Claudia. 1986. Monitoring costs and occupational segregation by sex: A historical analysis. *Journal of Labor Economics* 4:1–27.

Gordon, Donald F. 1974. A neoclassical theory of Keynesian unemployment. *Economic Inquiry* 12:431–59.

Green, Jerry R., and Nancy L. Stokey. 1983. A comparison of tournaments and contracts. *Journal of Political Economy* 91:349–64.

Greenwald, Bruce C. 1986. Adverse selection in the labor market. *Review of Economic Studies* 53:325–47.

Gronau, Reuben. 1988. Sex-related wage differentials and women's interrupted labor careers—The chicken or the egg. *Journal of Labor Economics* 6(3):277–301.

Groshen, Erica. 1991. The structure of the female/male wage differential: Is it who you are, what you do, or where you work? *Journal of Human Resources* 26:457–72.

Hall, Robert E. 1982. The importance of lifetime jobs in the U.S. economy. *American Economic Review* 72:716–24.

Hall, Robert E., and Edward Lazear. 1984. The excess sensitivity of layoffs and quits to demand. *Journal of Labor Economics* 2:233–57.

Harris, Milton, and Yoram Weiss. 1984. Job matching with finite horizon and risk aversion. *Journal of Political Economy* 92:758–59.

Holmstrom, Bengt. 1982a. Managerial incentive problems—A dynamic perspective. In *Essays in Economics and Management in Honor of Lars Wahlbeck*. Helsinki: Swedish School of Economics.

Holmstrom, Bengt. 1982b. Moral hazard in teams. *Bell Journal of Economics* 13:324–40.

Holmstrom, Bengt. 1979. Moral hazard and observability. *Bell Journal of Economics* 10:74–91.

Holmstrom, Bengt, and Paul Milgrom. 1991. Multi-task principal-agent analyses: Incentive contracts, asset ownership, and job design. *Journal of Law, Economics, and Organization* 7(special issue):24–52.

Hutchens, Robert M. 1989. Seniority, wages and productivity: A turbulent decade. *Journal of Economic Perspectives* 3:49–64.

Hutchens, Robert M. 1987. A test of Lazear's theory of delayed payment contracts. *Journal of Labor Economics* 5:S153–S170.

Ickes, Barry W., and Larry Samuelson. 1987. Job transfers and incentives in complex organizations: Thwarting the ratchet effect. *RAND Journal of Economics* 18:275–86.

Itoh, Hideshi. 1992. Job design and incentives in hierarchies with team production. Unpublished manuscript. Kyoto University.

Itoh, Hideshi. 1987. Information processing capacity of the firm. *Journal of the Japanese and International Economies* 1:299–326.

Jackson, Matthew, and Edward P. Lazear. 1991. Stock, options, and deferred compensation. In Ronald G. Ehrenberg, ed., *Research in Labor Economics*, vol. 12. Greenwich, CT: JAI Press, pp. 41–62.

Johnson, D. Gale. 1950. Resource allocation under share contracts. *Journal of Political Economy* 58:111–23.

Jovanovic, Boyan. 1979. Job matching and the theory of turnover. *Journal of Political Economy* 87:972–90.

Kahn, Charles, and Gur Huberman. 1988. Two-sided uncertainty and "up-or-out" contracts. *Journal of Labor Economics* 6:423–45.

Kandel, Eugene, and Edward P. Lazear. 1992. Peer pressure and partnerships. *Journal of Political Economy* 100(4):801–17.

Katz, Harry, Thomas Kochan, and Jeffrey Keefe. 1987. Industrial relations and productivity in the U.S. automobile industry. *Brookings Papers on Economic Activity* 3:685–727.

Kotlikoff, Lawrence. 1988. The relationship of productivity to age. In Rita Ricardo-Campbell and Edward Lazear, eds., *Issues in Contemporary Retirement*. Stanford, CA: Hoover Institution Press, pp. 100–131.

Knoeber, Charles R. 1989. A real game of chicken: Contracts, tournaments, and the production of broilers. *Journal of Law, Economics and Organization* 5:271–92.

Knoeber, Charles R., and Walter N. Thurman. 1994. Testing the theory of tournaments: An empirical analysis of broiler production. *Journal of Labor Economics* 12:155–79.

Lazear, Edward P. 1993. Incentives in a research environment. Working Paper E-93-4. The Hoover Institution. March.

Lazear, Edward P. 1992. The job as a concept. In William J. Bruns, Jr., ed., *Performance Measurement, Evaluation, and Incentives*. Boston: Harvard Business School Press, pp. 183–215.

Lazear, Edward P. 1990a. Job security provisions and employment. *Quarterly Journal of Economics* 105(3):699–726.

Lazear, Edward P. 1990b. The timing of raises and other payments. *Carnegie-Rochester Conference Series on Public Policy*, vol. 33 [Studies in Labor Economics in Honor of Walter Y. Oi], Allan H. Meltzer and Charles I. Plosser, eds. Amsterdam: Elsevier, pp. 13–48.

Lazear, Edward P. 1990c. Job security and unemployment. In Yoram Weiss and Gideon Fishelson, eds., *Advances in the Theory and Measurement of Unemployment*. London: Macmillan, pp. 245–67.

Lazear, Edward P. 1989. Pay equality and industrial politics. *Journal of Political Economy* 97:561–80.

Lazear, Edward P. 1988. Comment on Katz, Kochan, and Keefe, "Industrial Relations and Productivity in the U.S Automobile Industry." *Brookings Papers on Economic Activity* 3 (1987): Special Issue on Microeconomics, Martin Neil Baily and Clifford Winston, eds. Washington: Brookings Institution, pp. 716–20.

Lazear, Edward P. 1986a. Raids and offer matching. In Ronald Ehrenberg, ed., *Research in Labor Economics*, vol. 8. Greenwich, CT: JAI Press, pp. 141–65.

Lazear, Edward P. 1986b. Salaries and piece rates. *Journal of Business* 59:405–31.

Lazear, Edward P. 1985. Incentive effects of pensions. In David A. Wise, ed., *Pensions, Labor, and Individual Choice*. Chicago: University of Chicago Press for NBER, pp. 253–82.

Lazear, Edward P. 1983. Pensions as Severance Pay. In Zvi Bodie and John Shoven, eds., *Financial Aspects of the U.S. Pension System*. Chicago: University of Chicago Press for NBER, pp. 57–90.

Lazear, Edward P. 1982. Severance pay, pensions, and efficient mobility. NBER Working Paper 854. February.

Lazear, Edward P. 1981. Agency, earnings profiles, productivity, and hours restrictions. *American Economic Review* 71:606–20.

Lazear, Edward P. 1979. Why is there mandatory retirement? *Journal of Political Economy* 87:1261–64.

Lazear, Edward P., and Sherwin Rosen. 1990. Male-female wage differentials in job ladders. *Journal of Labor Economics* 8, pt 2:S106–S123.

Lazear, Edward P., and Sherwin Rosen. 1981. Rank-order tournaments as optimum labor contracts. *Journal of Political Economy* 89:841–64.

Lindbeck, Assar, and Dennis J. Snower. 1986. Wage setting, unemployment, and insider-outsider relations. *American Economic Review* 76:235–39.

MacLeod, Bentley, and James Malcomson. 1993. Motivation and Market Contracts. Working Paper. University of Montréal.

Main, Brian G. M., Charles A. O'Reilly, III, and James Wade. 1993. Top executives pay: Tournament or teamwork. *Journal of Labor Economics* (October):606–28.

Mayer, Thomas. 1960. The distribution of ability and earnings. *Review of Economics and Statistics* 42(2):189–95.

McCue, Kristin. 1994. Promotions and wage growth. *Journal of Labor Economics*, forthcoming.

Medoff, James, and Katharine Abraham. 1980. Experience, performance, and earnings. *Quarterly Journal of Economics* 95:703–36.

Milgrom, Paul R. 1988. Employment contracts, influence activities, and efficient organization design. *Journal of Political Economy* 96:42–60.

Milgrom, Paul, and John D. Roberts. 1992. *Economics Organization and Management*. Englewood Cliffs, NJ: Prentice-Hall.

Miller, Frederick H. 1982. Wages and establishment sizes. Ph.D. dissertation. University of Chicago.

Mincer, Jacob. 1974. *Schooling, Experience, and Earnings*. New York: Columbia University Press for NBER.

Mincer, Jacob. 1962. On-the-job training: Costs, returns, and some implications. *Journal of Political Economy* 70:S50–S79.

Mincer, Jacob, and Boyan Jovanovic. 1981. Labor mobility and wages. In Sherwin Rosen, ed., *Studies in Labor Markets*. Chicago: University of Chicago Press for NBER, pp. 21–64.

Mincer, Jacob, and Solomon Polachek. 1974. Family investments in human capital: Earnings of women. *Journal of Political Economy* 82:S76–S108.

Murphy, Kevin James. 1984. A theoretical and empirical investigation of managerial labor contracts. Ph.D. dissertation. University of Chicago.

Nalebuff, Barry J., and Joseph E. Stiglitz. 1983. Prizes and incentives: Toward a general theory of compensation and competition. *Bell Journal of Economics* 14:21–43.

Neumann, George R., and John P. Nelson. 1982. Safety regulation and firm size: Effects of the coal mine health and safety act of 1969. *Journal of Law and Economics* 25:183–99.

Pfeffer, Jeffrey. 1992. *Managing with Power: Politics and Influence in Organizations*. Boston: Harvard Business School Press.

Prendergast, Canice. 1992. Theory of Yes Men. Unpublished manuscript. University of Chicago.

Raff, Daniel M. G., and Lawrence H. Summers. 1987. Did Henry Ford pay efficiency wages? *Journal of Labor Economics* 5:S57–D86.

Reder, Melvin W. 1955. Theory of occupational wage differentials. *American Economic Review* 45:833–52.

Rosen, Sherwin. 1986. Prizes and incentives in elimination tournaments. *American Economic Review* 76:701–15.

Rosen, Sherwin. 1982. Authority, control, and the distribution of earnings. *Bell Journal of Economics* 13:311–23.

Rosen, Sherwin. 1974. Hedonic prices and implicit markets: Product differentiation in pure competition. *Journal of Political Economy* 82:34–55.

Rosen, Sherwin. 1972. Learning and experience in the labor market. *Journal of Human Resources* 7:326–42.

Ross, Stephen A. 1973. The economic theory of agency: The principal's problem. *American Economic Review* 63:134–39.

Rotemberg, Julio. 1993. Power in profit-maximizing organizations. Unpublished manuscript. Massachusetts Institute of Technology.

Sah, Raaj Kumar, and Joseph E. Stiglitz. 1986. The architecture of economic systems: Hierarchies and polyarchies. *American Economic Review* 76:716–27.

Salop, Steven, and David T. Sheffrin. 1983. Raising rivals' costs. *American Economic Review* 73:267–71.

Sattinger, Michael. 1980. *Capital and the Distribution of Labor Earnings*. Amsterdam: North-Holland.

Sicherman, Nachum. 1987. Occupational mobility and human capital theory. Ph.D. dissertation. Columbia University.

Siow, Aloysius. 1993. The organization of the market for professors. Unpublished draft. University of Toronto. November.

Smith, Adam. 1776. *An Inquiry into the Nature and Causes of the Wealth of Nations*. Oxford: Oxford University Press.

Spence, A. Michael. 1973. Job Market Signalling. *Quarterly Journal of Economics* 87:355–74.

Stiglitz, Joseph E. 1975. Incentives, risk, and information: Notes toward a theory of hierarchy. *Bell Journal of Economics and Management Science* 6:552–79.

Thaler, Richard, and Sherwin Rosen. 1976. The value of saving a life: Evidence from the labor market. In Nestor E. Terleckyj, ed., *Household Production and Consumption*. Studies in Income and Wealth 40. New York: Columbia University Press for NBER, pp. 265–97.

Thurow, Lester. 1992. Education and economic equality. *Public Interest* 28:66–81.

Topel, Robert H., and Michael Ward. 1992. Job mobility and the careers of young men. *Quarterly Journal of Economics* 107:441–79.

Tversky, Amos, and Daniel Kahneman. 1981. The framing of decisions and the psychology of choice. *Science* 211:453–58.

Index